LEEDS LIBRARY AND INFORMATION SERVICE

Rawdon Community Library
Micklefield Park
Rawdon
Leeds
LS19 6DF

D0238614

11/12/11

7 AUG 2012

Lib/1

LD 1506881 1

Amazing Gap Year Adventures

Inspirational true tales to guide you
on the journey of a lifetime

Tammy Cohen

JOHN BLAKE

Leeds Library and Information Service	
LD 1506887 1	
PromBooks	16/06/2008
910.2	£9.99
	SO53329/23C

Published by John Blake Publishing Ltd,
3 Bramber Court, 2 Bramber Road,
London W14 9PB, England

www.blake.co.uk

First published in paperback in 2007

ISBN 978 1 84454 345 8

All rights reserved. No part of this publication may be reproduced, stored
in a retrieval system, or in any form or by any means, without the prior
permission in writing of the publisher, nor be otherwise circulated in any
form of binding or cover other than that in which it is published and
without a similar condition including this condition being imposed on the
subsequent publisher.

British Library Cataloguing-in-Publication Data:

A catalogue record for this book is available from the British Library.

Design by www.envydesign.co.uk

Printed and bound in Great Britain by William Clowes Ltd, Beccles, Suffolk

1 3 5 7 9 10 8 6 4 2

© Text copyright Tammy Cohen 2007

Papers used by John Blake Publishing are natural, recyclable products made
from wood grown in sustainable forests. The manufacturing processes
conform to the environmental regulations of the country of origin.

Every attempt has been made to contact the relevant copyright-holders, but
some were unobtainable. We would be grateful if the appropriate people
could contact us.

For my mum

FOREWORD

THE MOST DANGEROUS THING IN LIFE IS NOT TO TAKE THE ADVENTURE

The clock is ticking and it's up to you whether you experience what life has to offer first hand, or from the comfort of the sofa as you sit on your arse watching it through the TV screen.

The simple question, therefore, is, 'What adventure is facing you right now, and will you have the bottle to take it?'

Unfortunately, life is full of people who reach the age of 60 and are full of regrets. 'I wish I had taken the opportunity to do that when I was young.' 'I always wanted to go to Australia.' Your aim in life should be to avoid being one of them.

So have I taken my adventures? Absolutely! Before the age of 22 I had travelled around the world, taken naked saunas at −30 degrees in Siberia (and yes, your 'bits' do freeze!) and I'd hitch-hiked across Canada and down through the US. If someone had told me at seventeen that I would have done all that by 22, I would have laughed. Am I unusual? Not at all. We see thousands of people doing this stuff every year on gapyear.com. Some do amazing things; David Parker, a diabetic, walked across

Australia in 69 days (a Guinness World Record); Ants and Jo drove a pink tuk-tuk from Bangkok to Brighton and the Fabes brothers cycled the length of Chile. These three events raised over £50,000 for their respective charities. All it took was a firm decision to do it.

This book is full of people with similar stories, the sort of people who inspire me to look at life in a different way. People who refused to follow the crowd, got off their backside and found some adventure in their lives. The pages are crammed full of life stories that, if you're not careful, you will never be able to tell unless you grab hold of the opportunity to get your butt off the couch and have a little bit of adventure yourself. This is less about achieving distance and filling your boasting book, more about the self-satisfied glow you get when you go to bed at night remembering what you have done.

The scary thing? These people are ordinary, just like you and me. The message is simple. If they can do it, so can you. If you are a sheep, put this book down now. If you're seeking inspiration and some advice on how to live out your dreams and really live life to the max, read on. And send me a postcard.

Tom Griffiths, founder of gapyear.com

PREFACE

Here are a few things I remember most clearly from the first two decades of my life... Sitting in a car in Sierra Leone with my parents, waiting patiently for a crocodile to cross the road in front of us; drinking my first-ever beer on a Californian hillside with a group of teenaged school friends while the lights of San Francisco glittered in the distance; getting off a cramped bus in Mexico after a 36-hour journey and seeing the crystal-clear Caribbean sea stretching endlessly, deliciously ahead.

See any pattern emerging here? No prizes for spotting that all these memories share one common thread – they all involve travel.

It might seem a bit, well, obvious but the thing about travel is that it involves Going Somewhere Different. And the thing about Somewhere Different is that everything is new and thrillingly unfamiliar – new surroundings, new people, new experiences. And when you're old and grey and huddled by the electric fire (which obviously won't be switched on as you'll have spent all the money you should have been saving for your pension and old-people's heating bills on round-the-world tickets and the world's biggest collection of sarongs), those are the things that you'll remember most vividly – the smells of a street market in Thailand, the colours of a Kenyan sunset.

Sadly, when I was of the right age, gap years – and just to be clear, for the purposes of this book we're talking about gap years involving time abroad, rather than those involving working in the kitchen appliances department at Debenhams during a year-off from full-time education – hadn't yet been invented. In fact, if graduates talked about a gap year back then, they were most likely to be referring to a Black Hole in their CV either caused by the mass genocide of several million braincells after one too many Happy Hours down the union bar, or a lost period of time spent playing Scrabble, visiting the dole office and smoking endless roll-ups on mustard-coloured draylon sofas.

So I have to admit to a few slight pangs of regret as I've been writing and researching this book. Okay, I'll come clean, I'm a seething mass of mean-spirited jealousy. I mean, given the chance, who in their right minds wouldn't prefer to be working with baby elephants in Sri Lanka or helping street kids in Brazil or trekking the Inca Trail to standing in the frozen-food aisle at Tesco's on a Friday night comparing the fat content of two different ready meals?

Trawling through the vast number of gap year websites, I've been amazed at the variety of experiences out there and the seemingly limitless inventiveness of the projects, placements and adventures on offer. Perversely, the world now seems to me to be both a bigger, more diverse place than ever before, but at the same time more intimate and more accessible. And at a time when extremist groups from all corners of the earth seem hell-bent on polarising the human race, it could be the stream of young travellers criss-crossing borders and continents, weaving networks of invisible threads in the dust and the mud who represent the best hope of keeping the world meshed together.

The simple truth is that travel makes us better, more empathetic, less judgemental people. Beryl Lee, whose inspirational daughter Stephanie was killed while working at a refugee camp on the Thai–Burmese border, told me that in spite of what happened, she'd encourage any young person to go on a gap year, and dissuade any parent from standing in their way. 'They've got to experience life and the world,' she says. 'The more people who go and do that, the better place the world will be.'

But, let's not go too over the top about the deeper global significance of gap years. Because basically there's only one real reason people take themselves off on gap years. They're a fantastic adventure. And sure, they might make you into a more rounded person and quadruple your knowledge of world affairs but more to the point, even in the most challenging of circumstances, they're also a laugh. In fact, say those who've been, they're about as much fun as you can have with a backpack on. Which is quite a lot really if you think about it.

After researching the subject for the last few months, the thing that really puzzles me most about gap years is why more people don't go on them. What on earth makes so many people think, 'Hmm, should I save up some money and then go off to Costa Rica to conserve the endangered turtle population, or should I sit in an office in Woking, pushing pens around a desk from nine until five? I know! I'll go for the Woking option!'

It may not seem like it when you're sat in some soulless library studying for impossible exams, or endlessly re-reading the bus timetable in some rain-drenched, god-forsaken bus shelter in a Mancunian suburb, but we've all hit the jackpot in the Lottery of Life. We've been lucky enough to be born into a relatively well-off democracy in peace-time. As a result of those two things, we have the luxury of choice. We have options. And with that comes a responsibility to exercise that choice – whether it's by voting out our least-favourite TV star on *I'm a Celebrity, Get Me Out of Here!* or by choosing our own destination in life rather than falling in with whatever comes along. If you only ever get one bite of the cherry, you might as well make it the biggest, greediest bite you can, wouldn't you say?

Writing this book has not only given me seriously numb fingers, it has also given me decidedly itchy feet. Every exotic website I've gazed at, every returned traveller I've talked to has reminded me that there's a vast, exuberant world out there, beyond the narrow confines of my personal comfort zone, just waiting to be explored.

In fact I wouldn't be at all surprised if I didn't take time off to recapture my lost gap year at some point in the future. So if you're on a bus going through Southern India or Bolivia or Zambia and you see an old biddy bent double under the weight of her amusingly old-fashioned rucksack, thumbing a ride by the side of the road with a shaky hand, don't forget to give her a cheery wave/lift/load of dosh.

And also don't forget, you're the lucky ones. You have the chance to do it all right now when you're young enough to wear those through-the-leg-tie-on Thai trousers without looking like an extra from the local Aladdin panto, and stay up all night dancing on the beach at Koh Phangan without needing a week and an intravenous drip-feed of caffeine to recover.

So what are you waiting for? You only live once (unless you're a Buddhist in which case you live loads of times, but could well come back as a dung beetle or something and won't have the same chances of foreign travel).

Do me a favour. Just do it. Okay?

ACKNOWLEDGEMENTS

I officially owe the following people a large vote of thanks and an even larger drink for helping with this book:

All the gappers, past and present, whose words bring the whole gap year experience to life

Nik Mann at gapyear.com whose dedication went above and beyond the call of duty

Tom Griffiths, also at gapyear.com, who neglected baby bathing duties in order to point me in the right direction

Jo Ash at GAP Activity Projects who came up with loads of good ideas for me to pass off as my own

Clive Hebard who raided his address book and bribed/ threatened his mates to come up with some cracking gap year tales

Wensley Clarkson who told me (nicely) when to start panicking

Michael, Otis, Jake and Billie who put up with a lot of very bad moods, particularly following the Great Computer-Meets-Magnet Disaster

CONTENTS

INTRODUCTION

So you're thinking of taking a gap year? This means you have one or more of the following: a) Very itchy feet; b) A sneaking suspicion that your A-level/end of university year exam results aren't exactly going to cause Dad to crack open that bottle of Châteauneuf du Pape he's been saving for a special celebration; c) No idea what to do with your life.

The good news is that none of these conditions is terminal. The even better news is that you've recognised that taking time out to go somewhere different will help you get your life into some sort of perspective (and give Dad a chance to calm down and write you back into his will).

At this stage, it might be just as well to clear up a few big gap year myths.

Myth Number One: A gap year is just filling in time while you wait for something else to happen. Er, no. The term 'gap' year is a total misnomer. I mean, what does 'gap' imply to you? Emptiness that needs randomly filling? A void that needs plugging with anything that comes to hand? That big hole that opens up between the train and the platform at Bank Tube station? The space between Madonna's two front teeth?

In its early days, the gap year might well have justified its 'absence of anything' name. It tended to be either a) the year where people who'd failed to get into their university of choice either retook exams or wrote endless begging letters to tutors explaining their momentary lapse in all-round general excellence; or b) the year when public school pupils stayed on an extra few months, commandeering the best corner of the common room, to take Oxbridge exams and generally lord it over everybody else before taking a five-month extended holiday.

So in actual fact, a gap year was once defined largely by its nothingness. But not any more. These days gap years are big business. And the business they are big in is the travel business. No longer is a gap year something you do when you really don't have anything else to do. A gap year is now something to aspire to, something to plan towards, something to dream about during the adolescent angst of exams and relationship break-ups and England sporting defeats. A gap year now is synonymous with adventure, with travel, with gaining new experiences and seeing the world.

Myth Number Two: A gap year is a year. Not so. If you break up from school or uni in June, your gap year is likely to run right through to September of the following year, giving you around fifteen months to divide between scrimping, saving and slaving and your dream trip. A voluntary placement can be anything from three weeks upwards. What you come to realise is that a gap year isn't something you measure in terms of time, but in terms of experience.

Stephanie Lee's mother (see Gap Year Casebook No. 2) was told that age wasn't a matter of years, but of amount accomplished, which is why her daughter died an old, old lady. The same principle holds true for gap years. The chapter on returning to reality is full of gappers exclaiming that even when they have been away for only four or five months, they've learned such a lot in that time that they've come back feeling completely altered, while at home nothing at all has changed. If you're going on a gap year, prepare to do some serious time-travelling!

Myth Number Three: A gap year is all about helping orphaned orang-utans or conserving rain forests. This particular myth stems largely from media fascination with Prince William's gap year experiences which, according to a recent report, spawned a whole new generation of worthy gappers and is hence known as the 'Prince William Effect'. 'Prince William has had a huge effect on the market for gap year travel, and students are flocking to Latin America,' said the report's author, Kate Simpson of the University of Newcastle-upon-Tyne, on thisistravel.co.uk. 'He seems to have almost single-handedly legitimised the gap year market. People are thinking if it's good enough for a future king, it must be okay for their children.'

But, you know, in the same way that not everyone would suit a great big crown and furry cape (so last season!), so volunteering won't be everyone's cup of tea.

An awful lot of the 200,000 eighteen- to twenty-five-year-olds who take a gap year opt to travel independently rather than do a 'worthy' placement (see Chapter 1 for the Backpacking-versus-Volunteering debate). Contrary to some popular opinion, neither option is 'wrong' and neither is 'cheating'. Luckily for us all, the world's a big enough place to encompass every different style and permutation of gap year, hair-do and alternative therapy involving bits of crystal on a string.

At the top of the list of gap destinations for those not planning a structured placement is Australia and New Zealand. According to a recent STA Travel online survey, 42% of those planning to take a gap year are set on heading Down Under. The next most popular destination is Latin America, which as we now know is fit for a king (or future king), followed by India and Asia, in joint third place.

The gap year industry is now bigger than, well, something very big. There are travel companies specialising in it, security companies offering safety courses on it, web sites, T-shirts, even a bumper sticker that says 'gappers do it with a backpack on' (actually I just made that up, but there really ought to be).

And of course, along with the surge in popularity has come increased media interest. The Gap Disaster Story is now a newspaper staple. Tragic but isolated incidents of backpackers killed in Thailand or kidnapped in Columbia are banded together under the type of headlines that induce panic attacks and life-long valium habits in already anxious parents. The fact is that, yes, bad things can and occasionally do happen on a gap year, but not very often. Not that scare-mongering gap year features don't serve a useful purpose, mind – they're very good wrapped around a portion of hot vinegary chips.

The problem is that the combination of gap year disaster stories and gap year myths is all too often enough to deter people from living out their gap year dreams. The same STA Travel survey of 14,000 students and young people found that a whopping 73% planned to take a gap year. However, previous studies indicate that, of that 73%, only around one fifth are likely go through with it. That leaves 80% who'll spend the rest of their life with a great big 'what if' echoing around their heads.

Misinformation has a lot to answer for. And that's really what this book tries to redress. From this combination of anecdotes, advice and insights from people who've already taken gap years plus live diary extracts from gapyear.com contributors who are currently living, or have recently lived, the gap year dream (with just the occasional minor nightmare thrown in), you'll be able to build up a true picture of what the gap year experience is really like.

Please be aware this is NOT a practical guide. Things that you WON'T learn from this book include:

- Where to buy the cheapest travel insurance
- Great places to stay in Kuala Lumpur
- How to arrange an urgent money transfer when you inadvertently get parted from your last £50 in a Thai lap-dancing establishment

What you WILL learn, hopefully, are things like:

- How it feels to say goodbye to your girlfriend at the airport
- Why an otherwise sane individual would part with a large wodge of cash to jump off a New Zealand cliff attached to a long bit of elastic. And then do it again... and again...
- The importance of taking an extra woolly when embarking on an epic Bolivian bus journey
- Oh, and you'll also learn a lot more than you probably wanted to about toilets and the stuff that goes in them

Most importantly, you'll learn that gap years are possible. They're not the preserve of rich kids, dare devils or people who have no intention of ever starting a career or paying back their student loans. Anyone with the capacity to earn some money and the imagination to dream of a world outside of their immediate environment can take a gap year.

Contributors to this book have worked in call centres, fast-food outlets and sports shops to raise money for their trips. They've done car boot sales, sat in baths of cat food and organised raffles. Some have gone straight from school, others from university and a few from relationship break-ups or career crises. They're young, not so young, flush, skint. Some want to save the world, others just to see it. They've had great moments, soul-destroying moments and moments so sublime they'll remember them for the rest of their lives. Some you'll be glad you'll never have to meet, others you'll want to take down the pub and buy a drink. They're normal, ordinary people. People like you.

Anyone can take a gap year. And you want to know something? Of all the people I spoke to for this book who'd taken one, even those where something had gone badly wrong, not one regretted having gone. That's a pretty good success rate. Think about it. And when you're done thinking, start doing. That's what they all did. And that's how come they've got such inspiring stories to tell, and amazing memories to share. Yes, there's a lot about toilets, but there's also a lot about friendships made, knowledge gained and places so magical they take your breath away.

If they can do it; if they can experience it; if they can lie in bed at night for years to come and relive every special moment of it, then so can you. And there's no time like now.

Chapter 1
DECIDING TO GO

'Should I stay or should I go now?
If I go there will be trouble
And if I stay it will be double.'
The Clash, 'Should I stay or should I go'

Making the decision to take a gap year is rarely a bolt-from-the-blue Isaac Newton apple-on-head moment of inspiration. Instead, it usually follows one of two scenarios:

ONE: THE CREEP-UP-ON-YOU-FROM-BEHIND SCENARIO

This is the one where you start dreaming about going off Somewhere Different as a kind of idle fantasy, in the same way you might fantasise about, say, exactly what proportion of your fortune you'll give to charity when you win the £15 million roll-over prize, or how it would be if you bumped into Johnny Depp while buying milk at your local Londis and he realised that, actually, what he'd been looking for all his life was a nice, normal, unaffected English girl...Whoops, sorry, got a bit carried away there. Anyway, once you've formed this fantasy in your head, you immediately start thinking of all the reasons it would never work. You'd never be able to raise the money; your parents would be traumatised; your guinea pig would die of a broken heart. But when you start working through all your objections, you find they're not actually as insurmountable as you first thought. You get offered a job in a call centre, with overtime! Your parents are delighted you want to expand your horizons! Your sister looks after your guinea pig for a fortnight and it instantly transfers its affections (ungrateful, fickle creature)! Gradually it dawns on you that, unlike the lottery fantasy or the Johnny Depp fantasy, the only thing standing between you and your Dream Trip, is you. You're snookered, mate.

TWO: THE TEQUILA SLAMMER SCENARIO

This one usually involves you and a couple of friends and a certain amount of alcohol. The dialogue might go something like this:

> YOU: I'm so bored of the same old same old. Wouldn't
> it be great to take off somewhere completely different?
> FRIEND A: Yeah, I've always wanted to go to
> Thailand because of the amazing Hindu temples. Oh,
> and the fit birds.
> YOU: And while we're at it, we could go on to
> Singapore and Vietnam, and Laos.
> FRIEND B: That's not a place, that's a bug.
> ALL IN UNISON: Let's do it!

Helen Woodward's decision to take off to Oz, with a three-day stopover in Singapore – originally a three-month escape-break that turned into a year-long adventure – closely followed the second scenario:

2

I decided to go to backpacking on the spur of the moment really, unlike most people who go off travelling. There was never really a plan – things just came together and it seemed the obvious thing to do. I hated my job at the time and was desperate for a change of scenery and direction. I'd been dumped by my fiancé, which seemed like the end of the world but really it was just the beginning! I was also about to come into some money as a result of signing my share of the house over to my ex – the house had doubled in value since we bought it two years earlier – this was the late eighties before the slump. What's more, I had a friend who was going off (supposedly for a year) around the world. As we sat in the pub one night I heard myself say, 'I'm coming with you.' The circumstances could not have been better, really. I still reckon it was kismet.

Whichever scenario you follow, the decision to take a gap year is usually closely followed by yet another decision (yes, folks – two life-changing decisions in close succession – and that from people who often haven't had to decide on anything more taxing than which sandwich filling in years). This second decision hinges on the all-important Backpacking-versus-Volunteering conundrum.

No subject inspires more controversy in gap year circles (imagine these to be not a little unlike crop circles – controversial, labyrinthine and popping up in the most unlikely places) than whether taking ten months to bum around Australia is a worthwhile use of a year out when you could be, say, saving the whale or teaching English to Vietnamese orphans.

Like many involved in gap year organisations, James Burton,

co-founder of Gap Sports, which runs sports initiatives in communities in the developing world, draws a clear distinction between 'self-centred' gap years and those which benefit others: 'We are encouraging people to do "productive gap years" – to put something back into the world.' Craftily, he points out that a worthier gap year is also going to look better on a CV. 'Employers and universities are going to be more impressed if someone shows initiative rather than sitting around on a beach listening to Bob Marley.'

Andrew Jones from Birkbeck College – which conducted a government-backed study into what constitutes a 'good' gap year as far as employers are concerned – concluded (as quoted in the *Guardian*, 27 July 2004):

> There is a clear differentiation between doing a structured placement and the people who go on extended holidays diving off the coast of Thailand. The research so far shows that the students who are doing the volunteering get an awful lot of good experiences. Employers are falling over themselves for these maturing skills, which they don't think universities necessarily add.

Such arguments incense Tom Griffiths, the founder of gapyear.com, author of *Before You Go* and often described as the 'Gap Year Guru'.

> Of course I'm all in favour of volunteering but saying that volunteering is somehow 'better' than travelling is a load of rubbish. Asking 'is it "better" to help sick children in an orphanage in Romania or sit in a bar in Thailand?' is just ridiculous. They're both valid. I

backpacked around the world at eighteen and, yeah, I sat on a lot of beaches – because they were amazing, brilliant beaches!

Neither does he buy the whole 'looks good on a CV' argument.

Employers have got wise to the fact that some gappers think they can use volunteering as a fast-track to a good job. They've stopped focusing on the question 'what did you do during your gap year?' and started asking instead 'how did you raise the money for it?' Someone who can say 'I held down two jobs for eighteen months to get the money to travel around South America for a year' is going to sound more impressive than someone who says 'Mummy and Daddy gave me the money to go and teach English in India for twelve weeks'. If you want to volunteer, that's fantastic, but make sure you're doing it because you want to, not because of who it might impress.

GOING THROUGH WITH IT

Tom Griffiths reckons that for every gapper teetering off through the departures gate under the weight of his outsized backpack, there are four gap year drop-outs. These are the four who were with you when you made the initial drunken decision to 'go for it', they were with you when you started planning all the exotic locations on your round-the-world trip, but somehow when it came to earning the dosh and organising the insurance, visas, injections and so on, they were nowhere to be seen. So how do you make sure you're in the 20% who live the dream, rather than the 80% who end up trying to bury it? Fiona Harrold, top life coach, author of *The 7 Rules of Success* (Hodder Mobius) and described as 'the most positive person alive', is one of those rare people who make you feel like anything is possible. She offers this five-point plan for fighting the 'wobblies' and seeing your gap year plans through:

1. Confront your fear

When faced with what seems like a big risk, like taking time off for a gap year, there'll be one ultimate fear running around your head, paralysing you and immobilising you from moving forward. The key is to identify that fear and confront it. Get a piece of paper and write out 'what is the worst thing that would happen if I did this?' Write down your fear. Once you see it written down, you might find it so irrational you can laugh it off. Or you may have to take it more seriously and take some action to ward it off. But once it's out of your head and down on paper, it's no longer running your life and you can start to control it, rather than the other way around.

2. Choose courage over confidence

When faced with a big change, most people make the mistake of waiting until they 'feel up to it' or 'feel more confident'. Big mistake! Might not happen! The real way to increase confidence is to do the very thing you're scared of, and then the confidence will kick in. If you wait for confidence to come first, trust me, it won't. Take the action and the confidence will follow.

3. Stop worrying about what other people will think

Peer pressure, when you start worrying about what other people will say about you or your decision, will stop you in your tracks. Take it apart, dismantle it and become your own person, someone who has authority over themselves. Remember it's you who dictates your life, not your family or friends. Write down on a piece of paper a list of people whose opinion you worry about. Now look carefully at those names. Some of them will be frankly ridiculous. Like you really care about what X thinks! Others will be less easy to dismiss. Practise saying to yourself out loud: 'I am the one who makes decisions about my life and accepts the consequences. I give myself permission to make change in my life and to take this risk'.

4. Assess the regret potential

It's widely agreed by those who work with people at the end of their lives, that the things you most regret are the things you didn't do, the opportunities you didn't take. Ask yourself this question: 'If I don't take this chance, is it something I'll regret not doing?' If it is, you'd better let go of the fear and do it, if not don't bother.

5. Remind yourself of your motivation

What was it in the first place that prompted you to consider making this change? Write out your initial motivation. Often it's easy to talk ourselves out of something so we lose our original enthusiasm and excitement. So if you wanted to go away because you couldn't stand the British weather any more, you might start thinking 'Hmm, well it stopped raining for half an hour yesterday, maybe it's not so bad after all' – and you lose sight of what was so important to you in the first place. Write out a list of your reasons for change and keep it with you, so that whenever you find yourself back-tracking, you can remind yourself of why you wanted to do this thing in the first place.

Backpackers also argue that a voluntary placement can limit the opportunities for spontaneous travel and that there's nothing to stop you Helping Good Causes as you come across them during your travels (although how many good causes you might come across in Surfers Paradise is open to argument).

Then there's the question of how much good voluntary placements really do. Recently a report appeared in *The Times* suggesting that gap year volunteers were the new colonialists and that the type of 'charity tourism' the newspaper claimed was operated by some gap year organisations actually does more harm that good to communities in the developing world by gearing their placements for the benefit of the volunteers rather than the communities they are supposedly helping. The report (of 15 August 2006) quoted Kate Simpson, visiting fellow at the University of Newcastle-upon-Tyne and the founder of ethicalvolunteering.com, saying: 'It's particularly problematic when volunteers are engaged to do the kind of work they would not be allowed to do in the UK. We wouldn't dream of having unskilled teenagers working in a hospital or teaching a class in the UK.'

Here, for those who can't be bothered to work out all the issues themselves, is a quick pros and cons guide to the Backpacking-versus-Volunteering debate:

Backpacking: Geographically flexible, with the chance to be spontaneous.

Volunteering: You're based in one place so you get to know a community.

Backpacking: Can be done according to your budget, incorporating periods of work if need be.

Volunteering: Can appear vastly expensive. However, the better the cause, the more likely you are to be able to get local businesses and groups to sponsor you.

Backpacking: You meet loads of like-minded people – usually because they come from the same country, even town as you.

Volunteering: You're much more likely to mix with locals from the community in which you're living.

Backpacking: Emails from a different country every week impress your mates back home.

Volunteering: Experience of helping on a worthwhile project might impress would-be employers.

WARNING: GAP YEARS CAN BE SERIOUSLY GOOD FOR YOUR CV!

STA Travel is the market leader in youth and student travel with over 25 years experience of helping send hundreds of thousands of gappers on their way. Says Jo Merridrew, STA Travel spokesperson:

Employers and universities value gap years! It shows you're adventurous, outgoing, single-minded and curious. It means you put yourself in positions where you have to show leadership, decision-making, negotiating and self-reliance, such as finding somewhere to stay in a strange town where you don't speak the language. A gap year will help you develop good communication skills and help you to learn to manage your finances. It also shows that you are motivated and have a desire to learn and adapt to different situations. All of these skills are invaluable in the workplace.

Know what, though? You could write out a million pros and cons, and ask a thousand different people's opinions (although it might be a life-long project should you decide to) but in the end there's only one thing that matters. What do *you* want? 'The best gap year is the gap year that's good for you,' says Tom Griffiths. 'Don't let anyone convince you otherwise.'

However you decide to structure your gap year, the decision to go for it is usually accompanied by a surge of wild excitement, swiftly followed by a feeling of faint nausea as you realise just what a monumental commitment you're making. 'I remember pinging and ponging (the movement not smelling!) from sheer excitement to excitement, fear, anticipation and a gut-wrenching sadness at the thought of leaving my mum and dad,' recalls returned gapper Liz Flenley.

And if the creeping nausea is starting to worry you, the bad news is that the worst is yet to come...

Once you've made all the dramatic life-changing decisions and nobly informed your nearest and dearest that you're stepping out into the great unknown and you might be some time, it's galling to realise that you're now expected to do all the boring stuff. Like sorting out insurance, visas, inoculations, passport photos... Sorry, have you nodded off already?

This is where a lot of people start to waver and suddenly remember prior arrangements they can't possibly cancel ('What? You meant 2007 to 2008? Oh no, that's when I'm washing my hair!'). The drop-out rate increases a zillion-fold when the word 'budget' creeps into the conversation and you add up exactly how much it'll cost to do that neat South America–Fiji–New Zealand–Australia trip complete with mountain climbing, skydiving and a tour of all the Lord of the Rings museums. Hmm, that's starting to add up to a lot of shelf-stacking hours at the local hypermarket, maybe a day-trip to Brighton might be more in order... Here's Tom Garrett's gapyear.com diary:

I have woken up some mornings thinking there is no way I can travel the world and come back in one piece. Not on my own, no way. I have, earlier in my plans, even considered not going and spending my money on something more sensible. It doesn't last long. The next morning I am back to normal, buzzing again and ready to take on the world, and more. The lack of faith in yourself is a weird emotion, but one you must ignore. Everyone goes through this feeling and to those who are feeling it now... Don't worry about it. It'll be all right. No worries.

Chapter 2
FINANCING YOUR TRIP

'Money is better than poverty – if only for financial reasons.'
Woody Allen

It's an annoying fact that, however great your motivation and
however hardened your resolve, foreign travel also requires an
extra element. Money. Lots of it. According to student travel
experts STA Travel, the cheapest round-the-world tickets start at
around £700. On top of that, they reckon, you should budget an
average of £30 per day of your trip, plus pack a credit card for
emergencies. That all adds up to... well, serious wonga. No
wonder so many people don't make it beyond the planning-in-
the-pub stage.

So how do you go about raising such a princely amount of
money? Well, there seem to be four main options: work;
fundraising; Mummy and Daddy; or a combination of all three.

WORK

Of these, naturally, getting a job is by far the most boring – but
in the long run definitely the most satisfying. Kirsten Spence
worked in a sports shop two nights a week and every weekend

during her last year at school to raise money for her Great Escape. Her gapyear.com diary from that time reads:

> I know I'm doing the right thing. Even if my family were in the financial situation to send me off on a very, very expensive gap year then I don't think I'd take them up on it, if I'm being honest. I think it would feel so much better to be across there having the time of my life and knowing I've worked hard for it. If I were across there knowing I could get any amount of money when I clicked my fingers and made a quick call to Daddy then I probably wouldn't appreciate the experiences as much.

Yes, getting a job can be difficult and demoralising. Suddenly you realise that nobody really cares that you were captain of the school debating team just as long as you're willing to make a tea round twice a day and don't mind nipping to Sainsbury's for the odd packet of Ginger Nuts. And your A grade in GCSE maths won't impress the customer who's been waiting six minutes for his Express Burger (joke: What do you say to a wannabe gapper with a job? 'Big Mac and fries, please'). But no matter how grim, there's nothing like the buzz of checking your bank account every payday and marking off another X hundred pounds from your Gap Year Target Fund. Tom Garrett again (gapyear.com):

> I spent a long four years paying off my debts and trying to save for this trip. I never thought it would come but finally I owed not a penny to anyone. I felt responsible, grown up and happy. Doing this was my Dare-to-Be-Great moment.

JUST THE JOB?

So you have to get a job to raise money. Big deal. I mean, loads of people work all the time. How hard can it be? Charlotte Martin reports on the shocking reality of the nine-to-five – and on learning to Just Say No to a new pair of shoes (gapyear.com).

When I took on this gap year I knew I would have to work to earn money – that goes without saying – but what I hadn't thought about was 'saving'. Truth being that when I have any money it burns a hole in my pocket and usually I have to spend, spend, spend. Okay, so I'm working as many hours as I can. Usually, after a long day at work, a trip to the pub for a few large glasses of wine (and then large amounts of JD) is in order. No chance when you are trying to save. I should be so bloody lucky!

I am so far impressed with my restraint, but God help me if I pass a shoe shop! Why do all the shops have to bring out their spring and summer ranges straight after Christmas? I know I'm not going to need pink leather strappy heels in Ecuador but what I would do... Back to reality, I have to buy mosquito nets and really attractive waterproofs!

It's not just the saving – it's the work itself! If this brief stint working full time in retail serves any purpose it is to demonstrate a) how much I never want to work in retail again; and b) that I want to find a career I enjoy and am passionate about (you can't be passionate about cushions and toilet brushes!).

And then there are the rude, arrogant, obnoxious customers – the ones who treat you like shit and still expect you to help them lift a box of porcelain off the top shelf, or want to know the price of something (despite the fact that it is priced on the bottom and they can't be bothered to turn it over and look!).

FUNDRAISING

What's a quick, easy way to raise money for a trip abroad? I know, I'll paint myself blue and hurl myself out of an aeroplane while simultaneously doing a sponsored 'hold my breath'. Genius!

The truth is, though, that gap year fundraising usually only works in conjunction with other means of financial support and, crucially, when the said gap year includes Worthy Deeds. Going round with a collecting bucket to fund a placement teaching orphans in Vietnam is a very different proposition from selling raffle tickets in support of a year in Australia drinking heavily, surfing a bit and trying to shag girls in bikinis.

Maureen Harrison, chair of fundraising group Capability Scotland, has this list of do's and don'ts for any potential gappers:

DO be clear in your own mind that this is a valid reason to fundraise. There should be a clear benefit to the community in which you will be working and that should be the paramount issue.

DON'T forget to seek permission to fundraise from the organisation you're working for. Here in Scotland this is important under the new Charities and Trustee Investment Act, but wherever you are, it's also likely to open doors to advice and support from the organisation itself.

DO make sure that you are very clear about all the financial arrangements first. That way both you and your possible supporters can decide whether this is a cause worthy of public support! Otherwise there is a great danger that people whom you approach may think that they will be financing a great year out for you.

DO explain the outcomes of your plan very clearly... the cause, and who will benefit and how in both the short and long term.

DO think carefully about how the people you are approaching would like to give and tailor your fundraising towards that.

DON'T forget to thank people properly for their contribution and ensure that you report on your progress.

Having said all that, fundraising is never going to be a walk in the park (not even a sponsored one wearing a chicken suit). With all the demands on people's compassion, not to mention their wallets, you've got to have a pretty compelling case for getting people to contribute to your cause. Either that, or a lot of good stuff to sell on eBay! Here's Heather Fitsell's eleventh-hour gapyear.com diary entry: 'Panic mode is setting in! Had a car boot sale and raised £45, sold some M&S vouchers = £60, flogged some old boyband posters = £160, sold some furniture = tbc (they've not collected it yet!).'

Car boot sales are an old favourite way of rustling up some extra dosh. But it can be disappointing to realise that people aren't prepared to pay big bucks for a bag of assorted odd socks and a Trivial Pursuit game in which all the questions are a decade out of date.

If you're doing your gap year through an organisation, that's usually the best source of fundraising advice. Tom Griffiths has counselled lots of despondent gappers still at base camp of their fundraising mountain.

> What I always try to convey is that it's easier than you think. The biggest hurdle is focusing on the number you're trying to hit – £3,000, £5,000. It sounds so unattainable. Instead try thinking small. If you're washing people's cars for £5 a time, you could wash ten cars a week, which gives you £50, which works out at £200 a month and nearly £2,500 a year. That's all from washing just two cars a night. If you break it right down like that, it's much easier to handle.
>
> Or try to think of ten things that will raise £100 each. Like you could shave your head for £100, or do twenty jobs for twenty people at £5 a go. Ten of those, and you've got £1,000.

Successful fundraising might also give you an edge when applying for jobs in the future, says Tom Griffiths:

> We had one girl who raised £1,200 by sitting in a bath of cat food for an hour [see Foxie 52's quote later in this chapter]. Imagine you're going for a job and there are two equal candidates, but the other one raised her travelling money by sitting in a bath of cat food. It's a brilliant talking point. Who do you think is going to get the job?

If you're intending to do Very Good Works while overseas, there are also organisations that might sponsor you while you're there. In her gapyear.com diary, Liz Ely explains how she's raising the funds for her teaching placement in India.

I chose Project Trust because they really seem to take an interest in their volunteers. You have to go to Coll (a Scottish island near Mull) for selection (which I did in October) and they decide over four days where is best for you to go. As an organisation they are really supportive, and they only send school leavers – so I would definitely recommend them to anyone who hasn't been travelling before, as they help you with everything – particularly the fundraising. Plus they are a charity so when you are trying to get money out of people you can use the 'it's for charity' line. Makes fundraising much easier – though there will always be some who accuse you of going on a year-long holiday!

I am currently still fundraising – I've got £2,800 so far. Am a bit panicky this week as I have a gig planned for next Thursday which I am seriously worried about (long story!). I'm also in the process of selling as much of my stuff (and many other people's stuff) as possible at a car boot.

Fundraising total update – £3,310! Surprise cheque £200 from a charitable trust, and £76 from Castleford Rotary! Only £540 to go now!

MUMMY AND DADDY

Getting your gap year paid for by doting parents may seem like the answer to all your prayers. And it may well be just that. In which case, the only course of action is to put up a pathetic show of resistance that you know will be overruled, smile gratefully and pocket the cheque. But, as you're queuing to set up your high-interest deposit account, you ought to be aware that there are two drawbacks to financing your trip from The Bank of Mum and Dad.

Drawback One: Everyone else will hate you

In the world of gap years, nothing is guaranteed to make you more unpopular more quickly than to let on that your parents are funding your overseas jaunt (well, apart from telling the fellow travellers with whom you're sharing a sleeper carriage on a four-day train journey about the nasty dose of amoebic dysentery you've just picked up – but that's another story). A long-running thread on the gapyear.com message board invites people to vent their spleen about anyone who uses the parental credit card as the magic carpet on which to jet around the world.

TERRY: I have met SO MANY people who came travelling with no money saved by themselves and so their parents are funding pretty much all their trip! I can't believe it! Even if my parents did have the money to do that for me, there is no way I would expect them to pay for my trip! You have to stand on your own two feet at some point; why wait? Anyway, it has really irritated me over the last few months. They are just thinking that money will always be there and mummy and daddy will help out. The thing that makes it even worse is that most of the money is spent on drink!

FOXIE 52: We were talking about going travelling next year. I'm frantically saving, working two jobs, all hours and doing fundraising. 'Rich' [travel buddy] rang me the other day all happy because her 'money problems' had been solved. When I asked how, she said her dad had given her £7,000! I couldn't believe it! I was so annoyed. I guess I'm jealous but it seems so easy for her! I mean, I worked as soon as I could legally hold a job (thirteen – paper-round, sixteen – waitressing).

'Rich' still hasn't got a job at the age of twenty-two. She pays no housekeeping or anything. By the way, 'Rich' told me she was being given £7,000 from her parents to go travelling on the same day I was told I was allowed to sit in a bath of cat food at work to try and get enough money just for my flights.

Naturally, all sorts of sayings involving gift horses (whatever they may be) and their mouths come into play here. I mean, if someone were to say, 'Instead of you getting up at 5 am every day to spend eight hours putting the lids on toothpaste tubes in an industrial estate just off the Birmingham ring-road for the next six months, why don't I just give you £5,000?' how many of us would really refuse?

But the fact is that most people don't have the parental financial cushion option and feel justifiably proud of themselves for being able to pay for those Tiger beers in that Goan bar with money they've earned themselves, rather than 'pocket money' doled out by Mum and Dad. Which brings me on to the other big disadvantage of parent-funded gap years...

Drawback Two: Your parents will have a say in what you spend your money on (and what they say will probably feature the word 'no')

Think about it. If you'd forked out a whole shedload of money on something, it would be very hard not to look upon it as a bit of an investment. Even if it's a gift, you're still going to feel slightly proprietorial about it. I mean, if you donated money to a charity, you'd feel entitled to check up on how the charity was spending your money, wouldn't you? And if it was spending your hard-earned dosh on little boxes embroidered with marijuana leaves or jumping off bridges attached to a bit of elastic, you might feel justified in voicing an objection or two. Amy Cox, now twenty-one, recalls:

> When my parents first agreed to pay half of my £4,000 total travelling costs, I was pretty much euphoric. But by the time I'd got two weeks into my trip and was fielding the millionth reproachful call on my mobile asking why I never called home and shouldn't I be going to a museum or something instead of sitting in yet another bar, I realised getting money from parents was a double-edged sword!

The ideal is probably the fourth option, to mix and match the three financing methods. Getting a job is a chore but it:

- Gives you a great sense of achievement
- Provides a taster of life in the Real World – so it's good for your CV
- Will probably be such a nasty shock that it'll make you appreciate your time away even more (as evidenced in the Gappers' Favourite Beach Game, 'What Would I Be Doing Now If I Was Back Home?' Oh yes, standing on Watford High Street in the rain handing out leaflets for passers-by to put straight in the bin).

Fundraising is a useful shortcut to a financial target, but rarely enough to fund an entire gap year project. Plus, if you want to go for the sponsorship/charity angle, you've got to be doing something Seriously Worthy.

Getting full funding from Mum and Dad has its pitfalls, as we've already discussed, but if you accept a proportion of your overall budget, you can retain more independence and still know that you've managed to raise the rest yourself. If you decide exactly where your parents' contribution is going – to cover the cost of flights, for example – you'll feel less accountable for the way you actually spend your time (and dosh) while you're away. And don't forget, many parents actually get a lot out of helping out financially. As their Little Darlings spread their tatty, unironed wings, it's a way for them to feel they're still connected to you, and that you still need them. Dani Webber, who funded her five months in Australia by working in telesales 'and hating every minute of it', recalls:

> When I first broke the news to my parents that I was planning a gap year, I was very quick to explain that I didn't want any money from them and was going to fund the whole thing myself. At the time it felt really important to me to be all self-sufficient. But after a while I realised that a) if I was going to save all the money myself I'd be working until I was 101; and b) my parents really, genuinely wanted to help. I think they ended up giving me around a fifth of the total cost – not so much that I felt completely indebted but enough to make them feel involved. I think if I'd done it all myself, they might have felt a bit redundant.

Chapter 3

PLANNING AND ORGANISING

'*A journey of a thousand miles begins with a single step.*'
Lao Tzu

'*Planning? What planning?*'
Helen Woodward, gapper

Who would ever read a section called 'Planning and Organising', hey? Isn't life supposed to be all about spontaneity and living for the moment? Well, yes... And no. While no one should plan their gap year with such military precision that it allows no space for the spur-of-the-moment opportunity ('Sorry, bus driver, I can't take a toilet break now, I haven't scheduled another one in until 11.42'), efficient planning in the early stages will save a lot of hassle in the long run, provide a much-needed structure for your trip, and reassure you and your nearest and dearest that there is indeed some method amidst the madness.

TIMING, SCHEDULING, ROUTES AND TICKETS
The first thing you have to plan is Where To Go. Now this might seem like a doddle when you're in the pub drawing routes on the

25

back of a packet of fags, but it's actually a lot harder than you think. There's the pesky question of budget, and whether you want to stick to travelling or work in a bit of volunteering, or even, dare one say it, think about getting a job while overseas. STA Travel's Jo Merredew stresses the importance of Thinking Things Through (those not familiar with this concept will just have to use their imaginations):

> It's really important to decide exactly what you want to get out of your year out and plan accordingly. Is your aim to see as much of the world as possible or perhaps settle in one country for a longer period to work, or try something new like voluntary or conservation work? Are you the adventurous type that likes to set yourself physical challenges? Do you plan to travel solo and make friends along the way or would you prefer to travel in a group? There are endless options available. Pre-trip planning advice is essential. It's really important to think about your travel budget and to research the countries that you will be visiting.

If you're doing the round-the-world option, there's also the question of arranging routes and stopovers that are both affordable and appealing. You fancy Thailand, but not Hong Kong. You wouldn't mind doing a bit of Fiji, but aren't bothered about Oz. This is where a good travel agent becomes your New Best Friend. You might even wish to marry them – there's a psychological syndrome where people fall in love with their doctor or counsellor or lawyer, in fact any authority figure who has helped them through a tricky time. So bear this in mind before you choose your travel agent – you wouldn't want to go falling in love with someone who looks like Shrek's less attractive cousin, even if he does know the entire Quantas Airlines timetable off by heart. And always remember, travel agents are only human (though estate agents on the other hand…) and occasionally you may even be able to teach them a thing or two, as Stef Marianski discovered (gapyear.com):

Okay, so today we decided to pay a visit to the travel agent to see what they could arrange. To be fair, they did the best they could for us, but what they do best is 'package holidays off the shelf' so I guess it was a bit of a shock when the girl we spoke to heard our plans… We walked in and I swear she was reaching for the 'Package tours in Oz' leaflets when we sat down. The look on her face when we started telling her the plan was priceless – we wanted to start from the beginning, so we were like…

'Okay, we want to start in Arkhangelsk and then go on to Murmansk…'

'…Okay… Erm… Could you spell those places for me, please?'

Anyway, we didn't really get anything done in the off-the-beaten-track department but she was very nice and basically said she could sort out a round-the-world ticket with four stops in each continent (except America where you get six) for £1,319, so that's not too bad at all… Anyway, obviously you can't get flights to Arkhangelsk and Murmansk on a RTW pass, because the only flights that go there are the kind on some cargo plane full of chickens flown by a dodgy Russian called Dimitri.

So she's going; 'The best thing is to book that sort of flight when you arrive in Russia.'

'...But you have to have your itinerary booked to get a visa.'

'Um, well I can find flights to... Madrid, Milan or Munich, but not Murmansk, I'm afraid.'

Anyway, the short story is that, lovely as the travel agent was, she could only really help with general stuff like flights and accommodation in the big cities, but not with any of the nitty gritty. Fair play to them, they specialise in packages and they're good at what they do, but I don't fancy being herded around like cattle in Russia!

TRAVELLER'S TOP TIP

Joe Bloomfield advises taking lots of spare passport photographs:

I had to hand two [passport pictures] over to get my visa for Cambodia. I used up all the other passport photos I'd taken with me, and only had those long-forgotten snowboard lift-pass photos in the back of my wallet to dig me out of an uncomfortable hole. I recommend you get yourself a fair few taken to avoid feeling like a twat handing over stupid ones like that. They're always handy to have. Better too many than too few.

It's very true that the best-laid plans can go horribly wrong, but it's also true that not laying any plans whatsoever makes it all too easy to drift off course, or more likely, find a zillion damn good reasons not to go at all. That's one of the reasons why, says Tom Griffiths, four out of five wannabe gappers never get further than the loitering-in-front-of-travel-agents'-windows stage.

People think it's too expensive – but often they haven't really looked into how much it is, and are surprised to find it's cheaper than they thought. Or they think there's too much to sort out, but there are plenty of tools available on the Internet to make it really easy for you. And really, if you can't be bothered to do two or three weeks of preparation for what will be a trip of a lifetime, you're not mature enough to go in the first place. You should enjoy planning for a gap year – after all, it's not as though you're prepping for an exam. You're getting organised for the biggest trip of your life.

The only way to progress from the woolly 'I know, let's go Somewhere' stage to the 'Back in a year, please water the yukka' stage is to make plans that you have no choice but to stick to. When my partner and I decided, over a couple of bottles of red wine, to take our three kids on a year out to Catalonia, we very soberly and intelligently wrote out a three-point plan on the back of the business card of the French bistro where we were at the time:

1. Get permission from school to take the kids away for a year. (Privately we were sure we'd fall at hurdle one. Everyone knows that getting permission to take children out of school in the UK is harder than a day pass out of Guantanamo Bay.)
2. Find people to rent one very shabby, run-down family home in north London for an exorbitant fee.
3. Contact all the magazines I was writing freelance for at the time to find out if it would be a problem for them if I moved base from, say, north London, to, say, Spain.

The great thing about check lists is that they allow you to experience a sense of purpose and efficiency, even while being quietly confident that number one on your list will prove so impossible that you'll never progress beyond it *through no fault of your own*. So imagine my horror when first number one was ticked off, then two, then three. 'Er, so there's nothing standing in our way, then?' we said queasily. 'Great.' Two months later we were standing on our balcony in the Spanish seaside town of Sitges, twenty minutes south of Barcelona, gazing out at the Mediterranean and congratulating ourselves on the best decision we ever made. But the point is, we'd never have gone through with it without a plan of action. Having a proper plan has huge benefits:

STAYING IN TOUCH

'Think about how you will keep in touch while you are away,' advises STA Travel's Jo Merredew. 'You can set up a travel journal online for free at www.statravel.co.uk and upload your photos and stories for all to view as you make your way around the world. You can also leave messages on your travel journal for friends and family to view and reply to you instantly.'

- You can make sure you tailor your itinerary towards what will look good on a CV and impress potential employers/university entrance panels. (Tip: writing '2006–2007 My friend and I spent five months drifting around Asia getting our tarot cards read on the beach and having yummy Indian head massages – oh, and I designed my own tattoo' won't really do you many favours.)

- You can save money and cut down on numerous pointless detours of the 'Damn, we forgot to do Vietnam. We'll have to go back' variety.

- It reassures your parents that you actually have some sensible idea of what you're doing. Even if you don't.

- It allows you to form some kind of notion of how much money you're going to need.

- It reduces the chances of you arriving in every country you visit at the exact time the monsoon season starts or the military coup which has been expected for months sparks off.

- It helps with sorting out insurance, visas, and medical stuff ('yes, I know I should have started taking my malaria pills weeks before, doc, but going to the home of the world's deadliest mosquito was just one of those spur-of-the-moment decisions').

BEST-LAID PLANS...

Planning Case-Study One: Helen Woodward

Our 'plan' was to fly to Singapore for a stopover and then on to Oz. My friend Lana had lined us up to stay in Brisbane with friends for a couple of weeks until we found our feet but then our schedule was entirely flexible. We had vague ideas of places we wanted to visit and where we might find work but we had no firm plan. We didn't have round-the-world tickets either – it was just one-way to Brisbane... with a three-day stopover in Singapore.

Planning Case-Study Two: Jane Yettram

We had initially planned to go in the spring. Then, talking to a well-travelled friend, we realised we'd be hitting some countries during monsoon – not a good idea. So I made a month-by-month weather chart of all the countries we planned to visit and devised the route according to both geography and the best time to travel. Because of this we brought our departure forward to November. And it worked really well.

We got advice on buying the ticket from a fantastic travel agent who, with the suggestion of a few overland sections, brought down the price hugely and really added to the experience of travel. It's worth phoning lots and listening to their suggestions as those with real knowledge are worth their weight in gold.

We also bought two separate single tickets rather than one round-the-world ticket. With a round-the-world ticket we would have had to use all sectors within a year of the first flight. With two singles (London to Brisbane, and Sydney to London – both with lots of stops) we could theoretically have been away for two years, though we returned after thirteen months. But it gave us the flexibility to stay a little longer.

We saved up for a long time before – mind you, we were older than pre-university gappers so had proper careers (both journalists) with proper salaries. We also owned a flat which we rented out, so we had security to return to. Plus we left some savings in an account for the first few months after our return.

I think it's important that your budget isn't too tight so

that you don't miss things because of money worries. For example, Jodphur Fort is a stunning place – really well cared for and preserved. Part of the reason for this is the 'high' entrance fee. (Well, it was a few quid each rather that the usual pennies in India.) We heard some travellers saying they wouldn't go as it was too expensive – but it's important to a) translate it back to your own currency and realise what good value it really is; and b) realise that this money is preserving history.

We prepared very thoroughly, and I think it paid off. The first country we visited was India and we read lots of travel books, fiction, etc. before we went so we knew exactly where we wanted to go – basically from Delhi, up to the mountains, back to Delhi for a wedding, Agra, Rajasthan, then a loop down south on the west and up the east to Varanasi and then on to Nepal. So we had a structure but deviated from it whenever new experiences arose.

Planning Case-Study Three: Ryan Price

We found it best to plan as much in advance of leaving as possible, especially in Asia. You can book almost everything on the Internet. The parts of the trip we did not book or plan ahead did not always happen! It can be difficult to access the Internet in some places, plus you don't want to spend whole days of the trip in Internet cafes. I also found it gave me something to do while I was staying in a lot (to save up) for the year before we left. Here's some of our hard-gained planning advice:

- If you need to cancel or change bookings we found that most places are quite flexible as long as you give as much notice as possible. We've only been charged a cancellation fee by one hotel for the whole trip! We've also changed flights very cheaply.
- I'd advise not being afraid to change plans if necessary. We changed a lot of our plans in Northern Queensland because the weather was bad – you don't want to be sat on a beach island, staying in a hut with limited cash if it is going to rain the whole time!
- A good guidebook (we are *Lonely Planet* addicts) is a must – they quickly become 'The Bible'.
- Credit cards are very handy, even if you just use them to guarantee booking and pay cash when you arrive. You'll also need them to book cheap flights only available on Internet.

VISAS

If you're ever at a loose end and want to while away a few hours or so, you could always amuse yourself by playing the Visa Game where you try to untangle all the red tape surrounding various visas to various countries. Particularly entertaining is the 'Thailand: Do You, Don't You?' game which involves asking as many different people as possible about whether you need a visa for Thailand and seeing how many completely different answers you can gather.

Thai Visa Opinion One: Joe Tuckwell

Okay, I'll start at the airport. When I arrived at the check-in desk at Heathrow I realised my travel agent had failed to tell me that I needed a visa for Thailand. I had understood that you can stay in Thailand for thirty days without one (which is true) but they wouldn't let me on the plane unless I had either a visa or an onward ticket, so I had to buy a plane ticket (which thankfully is fully refundable) for 200 quid! I wasn't a happy bunny. [gapyear.com diary]

Thai Visa Opinion Two: Liz Flenley

And then of course there's this visa malarky which I thought had been sorted. I had an email from the embassy in Hull saying that I DO need a tourist visa – so it looks like my friend and I are going to have to pull a sickie on Wednesday to go to Cardiff to get our visas.

Turns out that because we aren't flying out of Bangkok we need a tourist visa because we can't prove that we're leaving Thailand! Apparently there is no visa needed for tourist visas for people from 39 countries (of which the UK is one). This'll last you up to thirty days – but you have to provide an exit ticket. Does the ticket for my tour count as an exit ticket?

…Just an update on the visa situation. My friend and I both pulled a sickie on Wednesday and drove to Cardiff. We left at nine, allowing two hours for the journey and one hour to get lost and find the Royal Thai Consulate. We got to Cardiff at 11.15, and then all signs to Cardiff Bay vanished. So we drove around a roundabout for a wee while, finally deciding on popping to Tesco to ask for directions. Turns out that Cardiff Bay signs become 'the docks' signs and then change back to Cardiff Bay signs.

It was now 11.45 and we had fifteen minutes until

we had to be there, because although they shut at 12.30, they stop processing at twelve. Bearing in mind that although we were now on the right road to Cardiff Bay, we had no idea where Mount Stuart Square was! So panicking is a slight understatement of our emotions at that moment. We got stopped at every single red light imaginable.

We were stuck behind a white van man doing 20 mph and it was 11.55. We pulled over for directions again, and finally got to Mount Stuart Square. Yet this wasn't the end of it. My friend dropped me off and I ran up and down one side of the square frantically searching for number nine. It seemed that there was some weird portal malarky going on and every time I went past number three I'd magically end up at number eleven.

So I had to stop the third woman of the day, who looked equally as lost as I was, so I had very little hope that she could help me. Now you'd think that something that is called the Royal Thai Consulate would be huge, with a couple of flags outside, maybe a few Thai guards, a gold Buddha perhaps. No, no, no, no, no, no, no – try a piece of A4 paper stuck in the window of a tiny office, occupied by two very Welsh and quite old ladies.

I burst in gasping for breath at 12.05 and asked if I could have two tourist visas. I was then buried under a torrent of old Welsh lady abuse at the fact that she'd put all her stuff and equipment away, and that she stopped doing visas at twelve on the dot, that no one had come in all morning and now, would you believe it, Mavis, two girls come bursting in asking for two visas.

I apologised profusely, explaining we were leaving on Monday, that we'd come a long way, had been hopelessly lost and other such grovelling statements. At which point it was like watching Dr Jekyll become Mr Hyde (or the other way round since the doctor was the nice one) as she trundled over to her cupboard and took out one red folder. One red folder was all her stuff and equipment. But I wasn't going to say anything as she had agreed to do our visas.

So to cut a very long story not at all short, we got them. We have the stamps in our passports to prove it!

Thai Visa Opinion Three: Lara Hallam

On my itinerary I'm flying in to Bangkok and out via Singapore six weeks later. STA and Thomas Cook informed me I didn't need a visa while in Thailand as I wasn't planning to stay in Thailand for more than a month and I had an onward ticket. So I believed them as you would... Yet when I was at work, I read an article in one of those take-a-break-style magazines and it told a story of how a family got stuck in Thailand because they didn't get a visa before departure. Alarm bells rang.

So I came home and rang the Thai Embassy in London and was told you do need one! This is because we are flying out of Singapore and not Thailand. The embassy informed us you must fly in and out of Thailand in less than a month to not need one, and that Singapore is a different country so isn't valid under the onward-journey section. Very complicated. Anyway, so we sort out a visa – well, kind of...

You must enter the country within ninety days of the

issue date, so we can't get it before we go but instead will get it in Sydney when we're there. Problem solved! But for anyone who is unsure I would ring the embassies. It's better to pay an extra twenty quid than spend a night with the Thai police.

... Fast forward a few weeks...

Just to clarify about the Thailand visas: we had been informed that if you were not flying out of Thailand you had to get a tourist visa. For us this was not true; we got through the Thailand/Malaysia gate no problem. I don't want to say to everyone you don't need one, but speak to travellers on the way and go by their experiences, not always what the authorities say in the UK.

Those who get really good at the visa game could always move on to the advanced level – Russia. Here's Stef Marianski's experience (gapyear.com):

I realised my passport is a five-year one when they only accept ten-year ones (according to the site on Russian visas). Panic! I would need to get a new passport, with a new passport number, and change all my bookings to the new number... Absolute nightmare.

Anyway, I thought I'd chance it and take all my forms down to the Russian Embassy, and see if they'd notice. Dropped off the documents and got told to come back at 4 pm to pick up my visa. To cut it short, they didn't notice or if they did they didn't care – I went in, got asked a few questions about my trip by a dodgy looking Russian, but I think he was just suspicious cause I have a Polish name! Some might say they didn't notice, didn't care, whatever. As far as I'm concerned, I *totally* blagged it!

Russia is possibly the *hardest country in the world to get into*. Their visa system hasn't changed really since the Cold War. It has become slightly easier with the fall of communism BUT although communism is dead, the officials and authorities that upheld it are not. Policy has changed but the people who enforce it have not. And they are set in their ways. The way I see it, you have two options:

1. James-Bond-style parachute into the Kremlin at the dead of night from a spy plane. This is probably the easier of the two.
2. Get a Russian visa...

...Went to the Mongolian Embassy yesterday. Arrived two hours late, still got let in. The entire embassy is run by a friendly but rather scruffy looking Mongolian chap who was on his ciggie break when we arrived. We gave our ONE bit of paperwork to him and he didn't even look at it, just stamped it and *wham* we have Mongolian visas.

The Russian Embassy is a slightly different kettle of fish. Aside from having to be in the queue at 7 am to stand a chance of being let in that day, the Russian Embassy is like a bloody fortress, and they've got enough staff to run a small war. EVERYTHING on my SIX documents was scrutinised (except the one thing that could have screwed it up for me!). And then I was told to come back at 4 pm. I turned up at four and was seen promptly at five. More questions, and they finally gave up the visa. But they weren't happy!

INSURANCE

Okay, so now that you've seen the word 'insurance' flagged up in big letters on the page, for sure you've thrown this book down in disgust and started reading something more interesting, like the nutritional information on the back of the cereal packet. But the plain fact is that if, say, the spanking new backpack containing all your worldly belongings fails to materialise on the baggage carousel at Bangkok airport, or the elephant on which you are posing for amusing photos to send back home from India suddenly decides to demonstrate its new rolling-over technique with you still attached to its back, thus necessitating you to become intimately acquainted with the country's medical facilities, you'll suddenly discover that insurance is an endlessly fascinating subject – particularly if you neglected to procure any.

Tom Griffiths is full of the kind of insurance horror stories that send you flying into the arms of the nearest Lloyds broker.

> The big problem is that people think they don't need insurance because they're not going to take risks or jump out of planes, but we know of one girl who slipped off the kerb in Barcelona, breaking her ankle, and it cost her £3,000 to put it back together. Or there's the £9,000 forked out by the lad who fell off a donkey in Spain, or the £35,000 paid out by the girl who fell off a balcony in Turkey. At home, we're used to things happening for free. Abroad, someone has to foot the bill. And make no mistake about it, that someone will be you.

The moral of the story? Make sure you budget in a big whack for insurance – and make doubly sure you read the small print. 'Many policies cover you for riding a moped, for example,' says

Tom Griffiths. 'But only up to 50cc. So if the guy in the shop says, "Here's a better bike that can go faster," you'd better know that if you come off round the next bend, you're going to be paying for it.'

And it doesn't pay to be economical with the truth either. Tom says:

> If there's any chance at all that you might go skiing or bungee jumping, say, tell the insurers up front. A lot of people think they'll keep quiet because it might not happen, and even if it did they'd just pretend they hurt themselves some other way. But if you get taken to a hospital with a parachute attached to your back, trust me, they're going to know.

In her gapyear.com diary extract below, Sarah Cumming explains why she went for the comprehensive insurance quote before travelling to Asia. The extract takes on an added poignancy if you know that just weeks after taking out that insurance, Sarah was injured in the tsunami (see Gap Year Casebook Three in Chapter 16).

> Firstly, can I just say... 'travelling on a budget'!
>
> I don't know who thought of that clever idea but I think they were lying! I'm feeling a little bitter because I have just paid for my insurance and my credit card is feeling rather poorly. I suppose I could have shopped around a bit more but every time I read the small print on these cheaper policies I kept finding things that weren't covered and being the accident-prone person that I am, I didn't want to risk it. Also I'm lazy and couldn't be bothered.

TRAVELLER'S TOP TIP

Tom Griffiths advises customising your insurance:

Don't buy insurance off the shelf – it might include things you don't need that'll bump up the price. For example, being covered for 'travel delay' might be important if you're a business traveller, but for backpackers it usually just covers you for the cost of a few sandwiches at the airport. Similarly, 'cash replacement' might be great if you carry big amounts of cash around with you, but not so important if you rarely have more than a tenner on you. Remove clauses like that and you can save yourself some money.

Insurance becomes particularly mind-bogglingly important if you're considering doing feats of derring do, like dangling above the Antipodean equivalent of the Grand Canyon on a giant swing, or launching yourself down fast-moving rapids on a flimsy raft. Here's Vikki Anderton's gapyear.com diary:

Also been shopping around for insurance this week – work has been very, very quiet. Think I've managed to save myself around £50, which is about half my original quote! See, taking the time to trawl sites does pay off. The only thing you need to watch out for is the excess – some low premiums have high excesses; I saw one where they offered £100 money cover (not great) but the excess on it was £75! Just going through the small print and checking they'll cover me for jumping out of a perfectly serviceable plane with nothing but a silk sheet (and another person) strapped to my back!

MEDICAL STUFF

Be honest here. If you've even considered the possibility of falling ill abroad, I bet the image of your prone body lying under a mosquito net in some foreign hospital, sweating through a dangerous tropical fever while a local nurse, won over by your bravery, mops your noble brow, has crossed your mind. The English Patient meets Ernest Hemingway. The reality of being Ill Abroad, however, is far more likely to involve being permanently welded to a stinky shared toilet in a seedy hostel enjoying a second sighting of yesterday's curry while the Australian student wrestling team who are staying in the next dorm batter angrily on the door. It's at times like this you might start whimpering softly for your mummy and wish you'd taken up that place to study origami techniques at the University of Crappest Town in Britain, which you were offered through Clearing, instead of deferring to take a year out.

How much better, then, to reduce the risks of such a scenario by doing just a little bit of advance preparation.

Malaria pills

You can manage to tune into Celebrity Love Island at a set time each night and buy your lottery ticket before cut-off time on a Saturday evening, so why oh why can't you manage to schedule in taking a course of pills that could potentially save your life? Sarah Cummings's gapyear.com diary entry is fairly typical:

> Yesterday I realised that I had forgotten to start taking anti-malarials, in fact I forgot I even had them (thinking about it now, I'm still not sure where I've put them,

maybe in my hand luggage). I don't want to start taking them in case I get nasty side effects, but I think that's why I was supposed to start taking them now, in case I do react badly to them! Oh well, they have hospitals in Thailand, don't they?!

Last year almost 2,000 people returned to Britain with malaria and twelve of them died. According to the Department of Health, most cases resulted from people not taking the appropriate protective drugs. Don't let it be you. And don't, equally, rely on untested homeopathic malarial medicines to protect you. In 2005 the Health Protection Agency issued a warning due to people falling seriously ill when using homeopathic remedies. Its advisory committee on malaria said (as quoted in the *Guardian*, 14 July 2006): 'Herbal remedies have not been tested for their ability to prevent or treat malaria and are not licensed for these uses... There is no scientific proof that homeopathic remedies are effective in either preventing or treating malaria.'

So there's no way around it: if you're going to places that offer malaria-spreading mosquitoes on their list of attractions you have to take your medicine like a man (i.e. with a maximum of fuss and complaining). You might even find it's not as bad as you'd thought. 'I'd heard such a lot of horror stories about the side effects of malaria pills that I was disappointed to find I didn't get any,' complains gapper Zac Preston, currently somewhere in Southeast Asia. 'I did feel a little bit lightheaded, but that could have just been down to the fact I had a permanent hangover for the last three weeks before I left!'

TRAVELLER'S TOP TIP

Karen Golightly recommends shopping around for your medication:

Always check with the Medical Advisory Service for Travellers Abroad (www.masta.org) for the inoculations you may need and don't accept the first malaria meds your doctors offer. I believe many of them are highly ineffective and have nasty side effects. I used Malarone – most effective and least side effects/resistance. But pricey!

Injections

The headings just keep getting better and better don't they? Well, let's get straight to the point here (sorry): getting a needle jabbed into your bum might not be up there on your list of top-ten ways to spend a lunch hour, but it could save you a whole lot worse in the long run. Just make sure you get your timing right. Gapper Amy Lambert writes (gapyear.com):

Today I rang the pharmacy to see if my Japanese encephalitis vaccine had arrived, thinking that I had loads of time to have all three jabs. Only when I rang the doctors to book the appointments did I realise that it takes twenty-eight days, not twenty-one as I thought, and that I have to have my first jab tomorrow and my last one the morning before I leave to fit it all in!

Oh, and be aware that some medical personnel have been known to get a little power-crazed when armed with a very sharp object capable of reducing strapping young men to jellies. Zac Preston says:

> I thought I was pretty tough before I went in to see the Nurse From Hell for my injections. She started jabbing around in my arm like she was aerating a lawn and telling me off for having such 'teeny little veins'. Like it was my fault! I almost passed out but I don't know whether it was from pain or fear!

And even if you survive the sadistic staff, or the inept student nurse who has to try three times before she finds the 'right type of vein', fate might just still have an extra embarrassing surprise for you, as Stef Marianski discovered (gapyear.com):

> We were in the GP's waiting room and had just had the last in our course of jabs. We're standing in a packed-but-silent waiting room saying our goodbyes to the nice lady who gave us the jabs. She's going on a bit, telling us have fun, be careful, the usual. And just as soon as she'd disappeared she puts her head round the door and goes, 'Oh, and one more thing, don't forget to take plenty of CONDOMS!' We made a beeline for the door. I'm pretty sure the entire waiting room was in tears of laughter as soon as we were out of sight.

A SHORT WORD ABOUT PASSPORTS

Yes, I know, ridiculous idea! That someone could plan a major long-term trip and not check that their passport was valid! How stupid would that person have to be? Well, not as stupid as you'd think, judging by how many people (and not all of them a few sandwiches short of the full picnic either) turn up at the passport office in Victoria (yes, we know it's not officially allowed) to throw themselves upon the mercy of the passport issuers.

But your passport doesn't have to have expired to cause major headaches. Did you know, for example, that you won't be able to get into many non-EU countries unless you've more than six months left to go on your passport? Or, as Stef Marianski already said, that you're not supposed to get issued a Russian visa on a five-year passport?

Another important thing to bear in mind about passports when you're about to take off on a major trip where your passport will be your most valuable commodity, to be endlessly scrutinised and fingered by officialdom and new acquaintances alike, is that if the picture inside shows you before you grew into your ears, sporting your fourteen-year-old self's big hairdo and spotty forehead, you're going to spend a lot of your time away living in fear of that inevitable new buddy command: 'Let's have a look at your passport photo.'

Someone called Will Kommer once wisely commented that 'If you look like your passport photo, you're too ill to travel' and he had a fair point. So if you're going to get new passport pics done, for goodness sake pay the extra and get them done properly. Ideally by someone who has a camera that doesn't make you look like you're standing under the kind of fluorescent lighting favoured by customs officers intent on mounting an in-depth exploration of your luggage and, if possible, has taken photos before. Of people. Not used cars.

Chapter 4
PACKING

'When preparing to travel, lay out all your clothes and all your money. Then take half the clothes and twice the money.'
Susan Heller

Now, it might seem a little like overkill to devote a whole chapter to packing. I mean, what's there to say about throwing a few things into a bag, right? Dear Reader, there was once a time (oh carefree, happy day) when I thought the same as you. Now, having amassed more research on this topic than practically any other gap-year-related area, I have to tell you that if they offered university courses in packing, you'd be looking at a seven-year degree. With an additional 10,000-word dissertation.

For the wannabe gapper, the first indication of the anguish in store comes with the ritual of the Buying of the Backpack. A lot of pre-gappers foolishly look forward to this day with fevered anticipation believing it to represent a kind of rite of passage. 'See, it's not all a load of hot air. I'm actually going. I've bought the backpack!' It's not until they start trying the contraptions on that the first misgivings creep in. Lisa Hargreaves, whose 2005–2006 gap year took her right round the world, recalls:

I remember going into the shop and being gobsmacked at how big the things were. I was so completely clueless that I couldn't even get my arms through the straps without help – I had one arm in but the other was just flapping around behind me. Once I had it on, I was parading around feeling quite pleased with myself until the sales assistant said, 'Okay, now imagine that with the weight of a small child inside it.' I remember looking at myself in the mirror and thinking 'no way'.

SIX PACKING TIPS FROM STA TRAVEL'S JO MERREDEW

1. Line your rucksack with a heavy-duty bin liner to make it instantly waterproof
2. Take little padlocks to secure your rucksack (especially in dorm accommodation)
3. Swapping books means you don't fill your rucksack up 4. with reading material
4. Pack your bag and then halve it, and bring dark clothing as dirt won't show!
5. The best way to pack clothes is to roll them tightly
6. Take an alarm clock for those early-morning get-up calls, a torch and a Swiss Army knife

A handy general rule is that you should put as much effort into choosing a backpack as choosing a marriage partner. After all, the two of you are going to be wedded together for quite some time and need to know that you can put up with one another's idiosyncrasies. Mind you, the backpack has a few useful advantages over a marriage partner in that it rarely cares which side of the bed it sleeps on. And it never snores, picks the dry skin off the soles of its feet or uses the last square of loo roll without bothering to replace it. Trust me, selecting a backpack is like agreeing to an arranged marriage. Choose wisely and you will grow to love it. You might even surprise yourself by feeling a warm affection for it right from the start, like gapyear.com's Vix Carter:

> I'm really pleased with my bag, though, because it's so comfy. I would definitely recommend it to any females travelling. It's the Berghaus Sillhouette W. I also really like my Hanging Washbag from Lifeventure but I'm sure I will loathe all of it by the end of our travels!

But choosing a backpack is only the start of the traumatic process that is packing. Then comes the really agonising task of deciding what to put in it. Rarely can a simple decision have caused so much anguish among so many otherwise rational people. Here's Vix again: 'We have also attempted to pack our backpacks and realise that we will be going around Southeast Asia naked as we can't really fit any clothes in – will have a re-try nearer the time!'

The golden rule about packing, everyone will tell you, is to set out everything you're planning to take – and then halve it. But of course, some rules are meant to be broken, as Stewart Ferris, author of the inter-railing travel memoir *Don't Lean Out of the Window*, explains: 'Everyone knows the rule: get everything spread out on the floor that you would like to take with you, then discard the useless half of it. I recommend just taking the useless half so that your travels will be more of a challenge.'

Thank goodness you're all sensible, well-educated people who wouldn't think of leaving an important thing like packing until the last moment. Er, would you? Zac Preston confesses:

> I'll admit it, I was a useless twat when it came to packing. I'd started off being all responsible and putting all the things I was going to take with me in a neat pile in the corner of my bedroom, but by the night before when it came to putting Things in Bag, the neat pile had taken over most of the room – and there was a load of stuff I hadn't even thought of yet. I was still taking clothes out of the dirty laundry basket ten minutes before the taxi was due to take me to the airport!

Andy Frazer-Jones cut it equally fine (gapyear.com):

> It's quite weird how quickly the time has flown. I have been planning for ages and have all the kit, visas, insurance, injections, etc. and all that's left is the packing, which will probably be left to the day before. It's shocking how much effort is involved in planning a gap year and how much the bloody kit costs. Just when you think you have everything your mate reminds you of some other pointless poo that you don't really need but have to take. Still, better to be safe than sorry.

I WISH I'D KNOWN THEN...

Former travel writer Emily Barr, whose debut novel *Backpack* (Headline Books) became an international bestseller, gives the benefit of her vast experience of packing and overpacking...

> If I was going away tomorrow, my backpack would contain very few clothes (much better to buy them when you get there). Now that I'm in my thirties not my twenties, I would probably take nothing but a couple of Ghost dresses, which can be crumpled in a backpack and still look nice – but no matter what you leave with, you'll always end up in 'traveller' uniform of baggy cotton trousers and T-shirts. If you're going to warm countries, don't even think about any shoes other than flip-flops. I'd also take about four books, all of which I would swap after reading them. I love book-swaps you do while travelling: you end up reading things you would never otherwise have picked up. And a big diary and several pens.

Still, once you've put your things through the kind of rigorous selection procedure more usually employed by Sir Alan Sugar on *The Apprentice*, you're ready to rock and roll, right? Er, wrong actually. Because now you've actually got to work out a way of getting all those things in, defying all laws of physics which state that the volume of stuff going into a given receptacle should not exceed the capacity of said receptacle. Unless that receptacle is the Tardis. Vix, yet again (gapyear.com):

> The packing was harsh and I never want to do it again! I had three rounds with my bag of which the first two went to the bag. I'm pretty sure the third was a draw as I can now do my bag up but have approximately half an inch of spare room! Scotty is unsure of what he's put at the bottom of his bag but he thinks it's probably

important! We were both really trying to do the half-full thing, but it is impossible once you put in your sleeping bag and other essentials. So putting unnecessary items like clothes in takes the rest of the space. Maybe I should have gone for the next size up but then I probably would have filled that too!

TRAVELLER'S TOP TIP

Jane Yettram's packing essentials:

Packingwise, we did the usual work-out-what-you-need-then-halve-it. So we weren't overladen. A few little things really helped – string and a screw-in hook meant we could hang our mosquito net anywhere, flip-flops meant we could go in grubby showers and loos quite happily, and sheet sleeping bags took care of bare mattresses or dodgy bedding.

We also took a medical kit with needles and antibiotics, etc. Never needed the needles, thankfully, but the antibiotics cured a throat infection that felt as though my throat had been lacerated with glass.

FIVE USES FOR A SARONG

Sarongs are among the most versatile of items, and so well worth squishing into your backpack. Use your sarong as a:

- tablecloth for picnics
- towel for the beach

Packing

- modesty protector when needing to cover up to visit temples and holy sites
- curtain if on the bottom bunk in a hostel (tuck it under the mattress of the top bunk)
- sling for when you've forgotten to bring a bag and you've eight ice-cold cans of beer to carry down to the beach...

It often comes as quite a shock to gappers to realise that there's a true art form involved in packing for a long trip and sadly – unlike, say, tie-dye, or embalming dead cows in formaldehyde – it's not an art form that can be successfully mastered overnight. Here Sarah Cumming describes in her gapyear.com diary her Battle with the Bag:

I really hate packing! At the moment everything is heaped together, apart from my clothes, and it's just stuffed into my rucksack with no organisation at all and I would be quite happy to leave it that way. The only problem is that it's full and I haven't even decided what clothes I'm taking apart from the all-important bikini and flip-flops! The other small problem is that I can't lift it. Fine at the moment because I can drag it across the carpet and heave it up onto the check-in conveyor belt but what happens when I get to Hong Kong and I have to carry it from the airport to the hostel on my own? I think I'll have to do some serious practice this week...

I have now managed to pack, well, sort of. I did plan to try it several times and see which way was best and most comfortable, practical, etc. but in the end, once I put everything in, I didn't want to take it all out again! I know that everything is in there but I just can't remember where it all is but that's half the fun, I think. Let's play Find the Toothbrush. I also have to just note, that my rucksack only weighs 13kg! That's way under the limit and I'm quite impressed with myself – I really didn't think I'd be able to get all my possessions weighing less than 20kg. Unless, of course, that means I've left out something heavy and important.

TOP TWENTY PACKING TIPS

Former gapper (New Zealand, North Island, 1998) and GAP Activity Projects UK Marketing and PR Officer Jo Ash takes you through her top twenty packing tips:

1. A side-opening backpack is easier to use than a top-opening pack.
2. Put all the clothes you think you need on the bed then halve it – that's all you need to take!
3. Pack in reverse order – first in last out. Leave essentials near the top, so you can find them.
4. Pack everything in categories separately (start with a list – for example, clothes, equipment, first aid, etc.) and wrap EVERYTHING in clear plastic bags before it goes into the rucksack. It keeps it organised, waterproof, and you can use them again later for putting things in!
5. If you want to be really organised when starting out, use vacuum-packed bags to reduce bulky items such as towels and fleeces.

6. Ziplock bags are also good to keep your undies and other bits and pieces in.

7. Pack toilet roll and dirty underwear in the side pockets as thieves can easily open these. The same applies to the top pocket. Resist the temptation to store anything of any value here as you will be asking for trouble.

8. Leave heavy stuff like tents, hiking boots, radio, woolly sweater at the bottom. Keep spare underwear, a toothbrush, bottle of water and all-important documents (passport, travel insurance, driving licence, etc.) in hand luggage or a separate small backpack. Also make a note of important and emergency contact numbers and pack in a convenient place in your hand luggage.

9. The separate small backpack that may or may not attach to your large rucksack can then be used for day hikes and excursions.

10. Take a sleeping bag liner – this is handy when staying in hostels that provide the bedding, and it can be used on its own in hotter climes.

11. Take a sarong. They have a multitude of different uses, as well as the obvious it can serve as a sheet, towel, purse (knot your money into it), bag, etc.

12. Camping/sports towels are extremely small and lightweight, they take up less room, and they don't smell and can be packed damp.

13. Make sure you pack a first-aid kit – just in case. Check out the mini kits available which save on packing space.

14. Remove as much packaging as possible from things like toothpaste which have secondary packaging for

marketing, although if you do this with medicines make sure you take the medical information with you.

15. Shaving oil rather than shaving cream saves valuable storage space and weight. Put liquids into squashy plastic bottles then squeeze them to get the air out.

16. You can never have too many baby wipes.... or rolls of gaffer tape!

17. Fill shoes, cups, etc. with socks and undies!

18. Make sure you tie up all the loose straps on your backpack before it gets put into transit.

19. Take a good pocket guidebook, a journal to write in and a camera to really help you make the most of your trip.

Perhaps the most important thing to remember when packing is that, with the exception of your passports, tickets and money, everything else is replaceable. Towels, sarongs, shorts, T-shirts – you can get all of it at the market in Bangkok or on the beach in Goa, at a fraction of the price. So, as they say in American, don't sweat the small stuff. There'll be plenty of sweating to be done when the big stuff comes up, so go on, leave that third identical black vest behind. I dare you.

Chapter 5
EMOTIONS AND GOODBYES

'Don't like goodbyes, tears or sighs
I'm not too good at leaving time
I've got no taste for grieving time
No, no, not me.'
Truman Capote, 'Don't Like Goodbyes'

'Goodbyes are pants.'
Lisa Hargreaves, gapper

A strange phenomenon often afflicts pre-gappers as the countdown to leaving time progresses. The symptoms of this little-understood syndrome might include:

- Welling up with tears at the theme tune to Coronation Street
- Lingering in the biscuit aisle at Sainsbury's gazing dewily at the Rich Teas and Scottish shortbreads
- Belatedly realising that your home town, which you've spent years trying to get out of, actually has many, many hitherto unrecognised fine features

- Spending hours cataloguing all your old photos and letters
- Offering to help with the washing-up – unasked!
- Incessant mental playing of the 'Wonder How This Will Have Changed in a Year's Time' game

You'll look at your friends and family and, rather than disdaining their boring old nine-to-five routine, you'll envy them the security of knowing where they're going to be for the next, erm, twenty-five years or so. You'll curse the travel supplements in the Sunday papers, that huge poster of the tropical beach you used to gaze at every morning across the Northern Line platform, and even that nice Michael Palin for ever having convinced you that leaving the comforts of home to go thousands of miles carrying a bag the size of a small bus was a good idea.

When a gap year was just a twinkle in your eye, every other person you met was talking up the benefits of travel and waxing lyrical about how they'd found themselves during a five-day clay enema retreat in Southeast Asia. Now that you've taken the plunge and booked your tickets, everyone you meet is either full of their dazzling careers, or looks at you blankly and says something like: 'Nine months away? I could never do that, I'd miss my family/boyfriend/cat too much.'

And it doesn't help that most of your friends and acquaintances – and in particular, perfect strangers you meet on trains and buses – clearly think you're bonkers. Here's an extract from Liz Ely's gapyear.com diary:

Today I was sat on my own outside in the sunshine, minding my own business, drinking my overpriced bottle of Sprite, when some fat old warehouse geezer decided to witter on at me. He was so annoying and just wouldn't go away despite my unresponsiveness! He made some racist comments which I took as a good opportunity to talk about my going to India. So I told him that I was going to India for a year to work for a charity, to which he replied, 'Ah yes, I've got a niece who's just bought a house in New Zealand,' AS IF IT'S EXACTLY THE SAME THING! Moron. Many people in Yorkshire (and indeed probably all over England) seem to have two locations that they understand: 'here', which is very local, and 'over there', which could mean anywhere from Paris to Mozambique!

I'll tell you something else. If anyone else informs me that India is poor, I am going to deck them (or at least swear at them very loudly inside my head). The receptionist woman who was training me today very kindly informed me that India was in fact a rather poor country and I was 'in for some shocks'. Gee whizz, India is poor? That's news to me! I have only been planning my year there for ten months, guess I must have skipped the 'India is poor' chapter in my Lonely Planet guide, huh!

I just asked her if she'd ever been to India. (This was a much more subtle Louis Theroux-esque response than the easy option of being sarcastic. All those hours drooling over his *Weird Weekends* have really paid off!) It really stumped her, and after an awkward moment she replied, 'No, but my friend says it's like Gambia, and I've been to Gambia.' Oh, that's okay then, that definitely validates all the poo you've just been talking!

There's a phrase 'emotional rollercoaster'. You might want to incorporate that into your everyday vocabulary at this point because you'll be using it a lot from now on. One day you'll be crazed with excitement at the whole idea of foreign travel and feverishly looking up average rainfalls in El Salvador on the Net, and the next you'll be blubbing over an invite to your niece's fifth birthday party. In his gapyear.com diary, Tom Garrett says:

The emotional side is weird. Friends who have taken gap years have all told me about the mixed emotions that come and go from day to day during the build-up to the trip. I have woken up some mornings thinking there is no way I can travel the world and come back in one piece. Not on my own, no way. I have, earlier in my plans, even considered not going, and spending my money on something more sensible. It doesn't last long. The next morning I am back to normal, buzzing again and ready to take on the world, and more. The lack of faith in yourself is a weird emotion, but one you must ignore. Everyone goes through this feeling and to those who are feeling it now... Don't worry about it. It'll be alright. No worries.

The best thing you can do, I have found, is to keep talking to your friends about the trip. Don't bore them or anything (too much), just get the hype going and you will feel great. I have many friends who have either taken gaps or are going soon. Give me half an hour talking with them and I am ready to board the plane there and then...

... *Fast forward a couple of weeks...*

I had my ticket, had my plans, I felt sick. I really did. I felt physically sick. Suddenly, I didn't want anyone to mention it. It was like, if no one talks about it, it might go away. Again, this was that 'lack of faith' emotion returning and thankfully it went. I worry, still worry a lot actually, but don't really question if I can do it anymore.

The emotional build-up to departure day is intensified if you're leaving behind nearest and dearest who weren't exactly bowled over by the idea of you going in the first place – parents, for example.

Just for a moment, let's try looking at things from their point of view. For the last eighteen, twenty-one, twenty-five years they've invested heavily in The Project That Is You. If they've done their job properly (and paradoxically, you often find it's those who've been made to feel most secure in their home life that are most eager to leave it behind – presumably because they know it will always be there), you'll have been well looked after, educated and cared for. You'll have had holidays, Christmas presents and the kind of birthday parties where one child is always sick and another bursts into tears because he can't keep all the presents. Finally, this work in progress, this investment of time, money, patience, this cause of grey hairs and nervous twitches, is fully grown. And what's the first thing it does? Buggers off. No endless gratitude, no 'Now it's your turn to let me cook you a Sunday lunch for a change'. Just 'bye'. Oh, and 'I've come up a few quid short of my budget. Can you lend it to me? A couple of thousand ought to cover it...' When the gap year is triggered by either a failure to get appropriate exam grades, or a growing realisation that the University of Life ought to have been your first choice rather than Exeter, Bristol or East Anglia, parental emotions can run particularly high.

Gemma Lester was dreading telling her mum that she was deferring her university place so she could travel around Africa for eight months.

I come from a single-parent family where money was tight and my mum always made a really big deal out of how important education is. When I got into university she was so proud she even took out a congratulations ad in our local paper – just how embarrassing was that! So when I agreed to join two of my classmates travelling round Africa, I knew she'd be gutted.

I kept finding reasons not to tell her, like it was her birthday coming up and I didn't want to spoil it, or my grandma was in hospital and I didn't want to make things worse. In the end I just blurted it out one Saturday afternoon when we were out shopping. She was so disappointed, she actually cried. She calmed down after she realised I wasn't giving up my university place, just putting it on hold for a year, but I still felt awful – like I was letting her down.

And you know, parents, particularly badly trained ones, can keep a grudge going for just as long as you can, although their technique may differ in certain respects. For example, where you might employ the trusty flounce-out-of-the-door-and-slam-it-after-you strategy, your parents are more likely to favour the heavy-sighing-coupled-with-reproachful-gaze modus operandi, which can be pretty devastating if used effectively, as Zac Preston discovered:

When I screwed up my A-levels, my mum was all for me taking whatever I could get through Clearing, but I wanted time off to clear my head and reapply. We had a huge barney about it. After that she refused to take any interest in my travel plans and would pointedly leave the room any time my gap year came up in conversation. It took a couple of months and an awful lot of tea-making on my part before she relented.

Where affairs of the heart are involved, goodbyes can become even more torturous. Even the most understanding of romantic partners will have the odd twinge of doubt at the thought that their loved one will be sharing more quality time with his Leatherman than with her over the next few months, and these doubts tend to intensify as the leaving date approaches. Tom Garrett (gapyear.com):

> With the trip booked I had a bit of a time with my girlfriend. She was very upset that I was going, not that she didn't know for some time, but before it was booked it was something that we could both put in the backs of our minds. We didn't really need to address it, as it wasn't really happening. It is a strange thing to talk about. You see, no one really wins. If I had said I would stay, we would have got a house and some kids and a Ford Mondeo with a roof box. I would have been so miserable that it probably wouldn't have lasted anyway. If I went on the trip without really sorting things out, the bad emotions about each other would only come back to kick us both in the ass. It really is a difficult one.
>
> Many people said, 'Oh, you might as well split up then, there's no point in carrying it on.' I never did understand that one and do question the amount of faith there is in their own relationships. The good thing about us is we don't argue. We certainly don't agree on all the things that the other does (like all couples really), but we have never dictated what the other should do. We talked a lot and I think everything is cool. I am going, and she

is even coming out to Oz for a month in January time, which is great. Things are coming together.

Sex and relationships psychologist Dr Petra Boynton believes a partner's reaction to being told that their boyfriend or girlfriend is going abroad for an extended time is a pretty good indicator of the state of that relationship.

A really caring partner will say something like: 'I'll really miss you, but go for it and I'll be here when you get back.' They're sad they're losing you for a bit, but understand why you'd want to go. A more insecure or selfish partner won't be able to do that. They might undermine your plans by saying things like: 'It's great here, I'm earning loads of money, you're mad to want to fall a year behind.' Or they might try a bit of emotional blackmail, like threatening not to be there when you get back or acting not bothered.

When you're all hyped up about an exciting new venture, having a partner constantly trying to bring you down can leave you feeling as though you're permanently trapped in an edition of the *Trisha* show. Dr Petra advises trying to bring the issue out into the open.

TRAVELLER'S TOP TIP

Caroline North says, 'I've taken two separate gap years to South America and East Africa, three years apart, so I've had a bit of experience in saying goodbye. Here's my list of do's and don'ts.'

DO set up a webpage before going so that everyone knows

how they can keep in touch with you.

DON'T have a big leaving do the night before you go – you won't be in the mood to enjoy it.

DO drop hints at work about leaving presents. A light mosquito net or a travel diary or an mp3 player would be a lot more useful than the set of matching lime-green luggage I got from my first job (sorry, guys – nice thought!).

DON'T do emotional goodbyes at the airport. The first time I went away my then boyfriend came to see me off and I got so upset I was sick after going through passport control – not a good start!

It's hard for the partner being left behind. Even if the trip was something you'd planned before you met, it can still feel like a rejection. Why doesn't he want to be with me? How come she's not thinking 'I can't live without him'?

Tackle it by saying, 'What's going on? This seems to be about me going away and if there's a problem, let's talk about it. But let's be clear, I'm still going.' Ask them what they'd do if the tables were turned and they had the chance to go away. Don't even think about not going, no matter how much pressure they put on. This is a once-in-a-lifetime experience. And don't be tempted to come up with a solution like 'come with me'. It could be a recipe for disaster.

Many couples about to endure the Gap Year Separation are tempted to make an agreement to cover the time they're apart.

But Dr Petra advises caution before agreeing to things you might later regret.

> You might go away promising to text every night, but when you get there, you realise it's not possible. But the person left behind will hold you to it. Better to be non-specific. Say you'll be in touch regularly without specifying a particular day or time, or just decide on the best way to stay in touch: emails, texts, whatever. If you're making an agreement, it pays to be honest and confront issues that might be hard. Ask each other what would happen if either of you met someone else or decided the relationship wasn't working – would you want to confront it while away, or wait until you saw each other face to face?

For more on this subject, see Chapter 11: Love, Friends, Relationships. But you know, not everyone has the whole 'Parting Is Such Sweet Sorrow' experience. Indeed, some people, waiting in vain for the pangs of angst and grief to begin, have been known to feel rather cheated when they fail to materialise. Joe Bloomfield says (gapyear.com):

> There are now four days till we fly to New York and I feel strangely relaxed and almost indifferent. Is this usual? I don't know. I was expecting to feel overwhelmingly excited but to be honest I just feel normal. Eight months away from home and I feel less excited than before my last fortnight's holiday. That can't be right, can it?

There's almost a sense of disappointment if you aren't reduced to tears on at least a daily basis, as if your multi-stopover ticket should have included a good old bout of emotional turmoil along with the overnight stay in Dubai. Here's Charlotte Martin (gapyear.com):

> I've been saying goodbye to friends over the last week, which hasn't been as emotional as I thought, but I figured that I did most of the crying before they all went to uni – and now it's my turn to go away and have the time of my life! Not feeling smug about it at all! I know I'm going to miss them loads but with technology today and especially the wonder that is MSN, they are no distance at all!

To the relief of the shareholders in Hallmark Cards, most people don't manage to remain quite as unaffected. As the countdown goes from months to weeks and finally to days, it's not unusual to start experiencing a variety of physical symptoms – such as nausea, headaches and, of course, lock-jaw – from keeping your mouth set in a tight smile at all times. Because, of course, this is when well-meaning friends and work colleagues will be organising leaving parties for you. You'll probably be expected to make a speech or two, almost certainly including the line 'look how far I had to go to get away from you lot' or words to that effect. Then you'll have to chuckle over the personalised luggage straps they've bought you (just the thing for your backpack, not). And you'll definitely be expected to appear happy and excited, even if it feels like someone's using your insides to hone their needlepoint skills. Dani Webber recalls:

> My leaving do was absolutely the worst bit about the whole going-away thing. I'd been working in telesales with the same team of people for seven months and we were all really close. I think because we all hated the

work so much, we relied on each other a lot. So the day I left was really emotional. On one hand I was so relieved to be leaving, but on the other I knew how much I was going to miss everyone. When they handed me a guidebook with £200 in travellers cheques tucked inside I was so choked I couldn't speak. I just stood there with the cheques in my hand and my mouth wobbling like a lunatic!

However, the leaving party is but a dress rehearsal for the real gut-wrencher which, as anyone who has ever seen a Meg Ryan or Hugh Grant film will know, takes place at the airport, railway station or docks (or is that just in 1950s movies?) and involves a lot of quivering lower lips and anguished backward glances. Tom Garrett gamely took a whole posse of griefstricken loved ones to wave him off and ensure maximum tear-jerk potential (gapyear.com): 'The build-up to leaving was mad. I went to the airport with my family and friends and my girlfriend. I was starting to cry even before we said goodbye because I will miss them soooo much. I do already but I've got to get through it.'

The key to staging a really top-class airport scene, though, is timing. There's no point getting to the sniffling-into-a-hankie stage and then realising the plane is delayed by forty minutes and you're faced with sitting making small talk over an overpriced lukewarm cappuccino. Gapyear.com diarist Jenny Dodson reveals how she dealt with Departures Terminal Etiquette:

Once at the airport I checked in straight away and then it was just a waiting game till I could go through to departures. I spoke to my mum and brother one last time on the phone, which was nice, but saying goodbye to dad was so hard! We both cried and I just wanted to take him away with me, but I let go and walked through to departures.

No matter how old you get, you're never too grown up for a parent–child blub-in. Helen Woodward was twenty-seven when she decided to take an impromptu gap year with her friend Lana, following a painful relationship break-up. But did that stop her mum and dad from exercising their right to express the tugging of the parental heartstrings? Not a bit of it:

> Leaving was painful. We were to go by train from the Midlands to Heathrow. My mum couldn't bear to see me off. My dad took us to the train station and I think it was the first time I had ever seen a tear in his eye. Lana and I cried for at least twenty minutes on the train: it was real now – we had left home... and were heading off over the other side of the world. Lana was leaving a boyfriend behind, too, which made things even more difficult for her.

Farewells with boyfriends and girlfriends are always going to be fraught. Dr Petra Boynton recommends:

1. Anticipate it's going to be hard. Anticipate that your partner is going to feel rejected and try to save your excited conversations for other people.
2. Leave the airport decision to them. If they decide not to come to the airport to see you off – either because they can't face it or they're doing that passive-aggressive thing of trying to hurt you by not going – don't try to force it.

Chapter 6
CULTURE SHOCK

'I can't think of anything that excites a greater sense of childlike wonder than to be in a country where you are ignorant of almost everything.'
Bill Bryson

Remember in *ET* when the cute bug-eyed alien creature is coming to terms with finding itself in a wardrobe in a small human boy's bedroom, and everything it sees either fills it with wonder or frightens the living daylights out of it, causing it to run around shrieking and waving its arm-y things in the air? Well, that gives you some idea of how you'll feel on your arrival in whichever foreign destination you've decided on. One word of advice though: keep the running around shrieking and waving your arms in the air to a minimum, particularly when out in public. It's not a good look.

Any human behaviourist, a.k.a. compulsive nosy parker, will tell you that the natural response to the unknown or the unfamiliar is to feel threatened and on the defensive. Don't be alarmed if you find yourself doing any or all of the following while first adapting to a new place:

- Making a shrine next to your hotel/hostel bed with photos of family and little trinkets and mementos that remind you of home
- Spending more time in the nearest Internet cafe writing witty, happy emails to all your friends about how great it all is than exploring your new surroundings
- Feeling like you have the words 'Feel free to point and stare – I am an outsider' tattooed across your forehead
- Getting a headache from the effort of trying to look relaxed and entirely at ease rather than like a fresh-off-the-boat foreigner
- (If travelling alone) attaching yourself to happy family groups in pathetic, stalker-like fashion
- Feeling a stab of pure happiness at the familiar sight of the McDonald's golden arches

The fact is that waking up on that first morning to find yourself thousands of miles from home somewhere there's no PG Tips for breakfast and you can't throw bog roll down the toilet without causing a major international incident can be a real shock to the system, particularly if it's your first experience of travelling alone. Serial gapper James Whitaker says:

Culture shock has hit me, with varying degrees of intensity, on all of my trips, particularly to the less developed world. It is a given of travelling, particularly for the first time, that you will spend the first day or so feeling completely out at sea; isolated, lonely, and wondering why you ever bothered leaving England. I have heard of people who are generally very outgoing and confident, arriving in a new country, usually on their first major trip abroad, and spending days (literally) holed up in their first hotel room, not wanting to go out or meet anyone or do anything.

When I left university I took a spur of the moment job teaching English in a private language school in what was then an obscure city in southern Spain. The fact that I'd a) never been to Spain, b) never taught English, and c) not bothered to learn a single word of Spanish didn't strike me as being at all an impediment to what I was sure would be a jolly good wheeze – until, that is, I got up on the first morning, realised I couldn't even order a piece of toast in a cafe without the humiliation of miming it out first, and crumpled into a snivelling, self-pitying heap. For three days I stayed in my hotel room, living off a packet of digestive biscuits I'd bought at the airport and making increasingly incoherent, choked phone calls home.

Until you've experienced it, nothing can quite prepare you for the shock of realising that what's perfectly normal at home *isn't normal everywhere else*! And in fact there are whole communities, whole countries, indeed, doing things in a completely bizarre and inexplicable fashion *and believing that they're the normal ones*! And what's even worse, thinking you're the odd one for not doing things in exactly the same way they do. Novelist Emily Barr recalls:

I remember my first morning in Asia, in Ho Chi Minh City, when it took me half an hour to get across the road because I didn't dare follow everyone else and just step out and let the motorbikes and cars and bicycles and buses swerve around me. In the end, inevitably, a kind passer-by took me by the arm and guided me over as if I were blind. I can still remember the sense of achievement I got the first time I did it on my own.

TRAVELLER'S TOP TIP

Karen Golightly says to forget the moral high ground:

So long as you read up on where you're going you can avoid most culture shock. Depending on your principles, you will find some local ways harder to deal with – for example, the treatment of animals and women. If you consider yourself to be liberated, prepare to be shocked by some things you'll see but try to be respectful of others' cultures. England isn't an empire anymore and there's a fine line between 'educating' the locals and brow beating.

Even the most prepared and well-researched gappers can find themselves flummoxed to discover that, though they might have swotted up on all the sights of interest in the guidebook, they didn't realise that the main sight of interest would be them! But anyone exploring the less touristy destinations should be prepared to find themselves the centre of attention. Travel journalist Rupert Mellor has had his share of being pointed and giggled at. But enough about his private life, here's his take on what to expect when travelling:

Culture shock can strike in many contexts – diet, language, customs, climate – so a little research into local life in your destination will give you a feel for just how foreign life there will feel, and also how much of a novelty you'll be. The rough rule is, the less familiar foreign faces are where you'll be, the more attention you will warrant. Very touristy areas are very at ease with foreign visitors, although it's worth watching out for resentment and tourist-targeted crime in such places. Your comparitive level of wealth can also colour your interactions with local people. Whether attention is a good or bad thing is down to the ways of your host location, and how you feel about standing out in the crowd. You can help yourself feel established in a new place by setting up some elements of routine – a favourite breakfast spot, for example, where you'll soon be familiar to the staff and can make friends to give you local advice and opinions, can help root you in your new situation. Stay calm and unflappable if overwhelmed by people offering you services, advice, friendship – don't be rushed into anything, and take the time to find out what the norms are.

TRAVELLER'S TOP TIP

'Be aware you'll be as big a shock to them as they are to you,' Sarah Epton says. 'I nearly caused a three-motorbike-and-a-tuk-tuk pile-up at a set of traffic lights in Bangkok. The motorbike driver had never seen such huge breasts. They simply don't grow them that large in Southeast Asia!'

For many gappers, often embarking on their first experience of long-haul travel, it's the poverty that provides the greatest initial shock. Most of us have been asked for money in the UK, but being surrounded by a throng of beggars, all jostling you for money, is a very different experience. Here's Liz Ely's gapyear.com diary:

As we left the airport I had my first disturbing 'Indian poverty' experience. We were loading all our stuff into Bharavi's Jeep and some women in black robes were mumbling in low voices, tapping us – asking for money. Bear in mind that it was four in the morning, I felt incredibly tired, so instead of feeling the usual mixture of guilt, pity and irritation (how I now feel about beggars), I felt very uneasy; they seemed eerie to me, almost demonic in their black robes. Even now I still find women who are completely shrouded in black disturbing.

Joe Bloomfield won't forget the impact of his first up-close and very personal encounter with poverty on his trip to Cambodia, recounted in his gapyear.com diary.

I got to Siem Reap at about ten o'clock at night, got to my hotel and put my head down. In the morning, I got up and went out for a look around town. As soon as I set foot outside the hotel, little kids of no more than five came up to me asking for money. I tried to wave them off but they just followed me around. As soon as one gave up, another one tried their luck. I wasn't prepared for it at all. After about twenty minutes' wandering around, a guy of about forty with his shirt open stepped out in front of me from behind a rack of clothes and blocked my path.

'Hello, mister!' he said in a cheery voice. I looked into his face and greeted him with a smile. Small scars twisted his features in unusual directions. My gaze drifted down to his chest. More scars, bigger this time.

'Lan My!' he said, as I noticed for the first time the stumps where his arms should have been. 'Lan My! BOOM!'

At this point he threw his stumps out to their extremities in an attempt to demonstrate the size of the blast caused by the mine. I recoiled in shock and, I am ashamed to say, disgust.

'Money for food?' he asked me, in a timid voice. I looked back into his face and he could no longer meet my eye. It struck me then that here was a fiercely proud man, reduced to begging tourists for enough money to stop him being hungry. I thought about getting a note out, realised I couldn't give it to him without tucking it in between his teeth, and got embarrassed and flustered. I turned around and fled for the sanctity of my hotel room, where I had the nice Western luxuries of cable TV and air conditioning waiting for me, to take my mind off the shock of what had just happened.

I sat in my room and felt guilty as I thought about the appalling way I had just handled the situation. I just hadn't been prepared for anything like that at all, and made a resolve to be friendly and pleasant to the beggars in future. I wondered about how valid the arguments for not giving money to beggars are when you come face to face with someone as wretched as that, whose fate was brought about by a war whose politics he probably never really even knew about, let alone cared for. He was the first of many – far, far too many – land-mine victims I saw on the streets of Cambodia, and I was a lot more understanding to them from then on.

Poverty is always a difficult one to confront, no matter how prepared you think you are. You'll feel upset, but above all you'll feel impotent. 'But you aren't powerless,' argues gapyear.com's Tom Griffiths. 'If you're really affected by what you see, you'll come home and you'll educate people and that's how things get changed.'

It's not only poverty that upsets many gappers, but also what we perceive as injustice. Caste systems, aggression towards children and suppression of women's rights can come as a huge shock. Tom says:

> We get girls coming back outraged about the treatment of women in countries they've visited. What you have to understand is that you're not there to judge. You have to try to understand the situation rather than passing judgement. After all, a visitor to the UK may find some of the things we have here disgusting. Who are we to judge? At the very least, you'll come back home and feel privileged to live here.

Sometimes the shock of being in a new place doesn't come from how different it is from what we're used to, but from how different it is from our own expectations. It's like Americans who come to London expecting it to be like it is in the Bridget Jones movies and are taken aback to find that, rather than lounging about in gorgeous loft apartments above Bond Street, your average Londoner is far more likely to live in a pebble-dashed semi off the North Circular. So we're horrified by the rubbish on the beaches in Goa and the fact that not every South Pacific islander greets you with a wide smile before placing a garland of flowers around your neck. Why oh why can't places look just the way they do in the movies? Isn't there a law that says they have to? Stef Marianski was less than impressed by his first day in Moscow (gapyear.com):

Culture Shock

We arrived in Moscow yesterday by train. First impressions: it's grim. To be honest it seems a bit over-hyped – there's not much to do except the Kremlin (which was closed today), and the hostel is absolutely bleak – no hot water, tenth floor of a dodgy block of flats on the outskirts of Moscow. The first person we saw when we arrived was a disgruntled Hawaiian guy who explained that the place 'sucks', his room-mates had gone off with the room key eleven hours ago and loads of people have had money stolen – makes me feel like less of a muppet for bringing that Pacsafe mesh!

TRAVELLER'S TOP TIP

Carry lots of small change, advises Sheldon Warnick:

Change a dollar or five dollars into small change and keep it in your pockets. If you're in a poor country like Cambodia, you've got to expect to have a lot of people coming up to you asking for money. The thing is just to talk to them like you would anyone else. There's not the same stigma in begging in a country like that because everyone's so poor they all understand that the beggars can't help it. If you give them even the equivalent of 2p, they can do something with it. What can you do with it?

Even the reality of Hollywood, surely one of the most instantly familiar places on earth as the setting of thousands of TV shows and movies, can prove a shock, as Hannah Bailey discovered on the first leg of her gap year (gapyear.com):

I arrived in LA on Wednesday during the afternoon. It was quite a shock, I wasn't expecting as much concrete as there was. So many cars and such a mission to cross the road. I arrived at the Howard Johnson hotel. I had a double room and ensuite just so I could get accustomed to travelling by myself. I watched Sky and then rang home. On Thursday I went into town. I first arrived at Venice Beach. I watched a man smash glass bottles on his head and then headed down to the beach front. Then an old lady sitting at the side of the street with all of her belongings in a trolley started hurling abuse at me. I left LA on the Friday. I definitely would not recommend any more than two nights there.

Real culture shock goes way beyond the visual – all the senses get a battering. The air smells different, familiar foods taste different, background noises are different. EVERYTHING is different. Here's Liz Ely again (gapyear.com):

When I first arrived in India it was the smell that hit me the most, not the heat or the poverty as I was expecting, but this incredible mixture of food, incense, sweat, shit and something else that fills the air. You can hide from the noise and shut yourself off from the beggars but the smell surrounds you, filling your lungs every time you breathe.

The great thing about culture shock, though, is that it's fleeting. Like any shock, once it wears off a bit and you've had a chance to evaluate whatever caused it in the first place, you'll rediscover the universal truth that you knew all along (because we're all taught it at circle time in primary school these days), that what's different doesn't have to be frightening. And in fact it's only through seeking out what's different that we continue to learn and grow (sorry, came over all 'Thought For the Day' there).

Former travel writer Emily Barr has been all over the world:

Culture shock is the best part of travelling! I love culture shock. There's nothing as thrilling as arriving in, say, China, and instantly feeling you're in a new universe. It's strange when people stare at you wherever you go, but in a good way. There's a little adrenaline rush to be had from knowing the name of the station where you want to get off the train, but not being able to read the signs, so being totally dependent on strangers to help you out. I think that being overwhelmed by new sights and sounds and smells does everyone a huge amount of good. It's good to be a fish out of water. It's fantastic to have to find your way around. Likewise, it's exciting to order something off a menu you can't understand, and find out that you've ordered the right thing, or to bargain successfully at a market. Also, however much we in the West might know about poverty, slums and starving children, when you see the reality, something changes inside you. It does everyone good. The only bad thing, I think, is that culture shock can make some people scared, so they put up barriers and become stereotypical arrogant Westerners. There's nothing more depressing than hearing a white traveller in a shouting match with a rickshaw driver over the equivalent of 5p. It's important to try to keep a sense of perspective... My other pet hate is the 'you can't give to beggars because it just upholds the system' argument. Yes, that's true, theoretically, but if someone is literally starving in front of you, and you have a pocket full of coins, of course you should help them out. Nobody is going to give to every beggar every time, but it's easy to see when they're truly desperate.

TRAVELLER'S TOP TIP

Tom Griffiths advocates doing your research:

With the advent of the Internet, there's no excuse for not being prepared for what you'll find. If you're going to Indonesia, you should have a rough idea of what Indonesia looks like. And you should also get clued up about local customs in the places you're visiting. In some countries it's rude to show the soles of your feet – you try getting into a hammock without doing that!

Of course, sometimes the most shocking thing about a new culture is... when it's not shocking at all (nor, arguably, could it be classed as culture in some cases). Ryan Price was a little disappointed by the lack of culture shock when he arrived in Sydney.

There's not much culture shock in Australia! Sometimes it's hard to believe that you are on the other side of the world. My sister said she felt odd when she arrived because she had been on a plane for so long and had travelled 'over' so many places and yet she ended up somewhere very similar to home – but not quite!

Chapter 7
FOOD, TOILETS AND OTHER BASIC STUFF

'Travel is glamorous only in retrospect.'
Paul Theroux

We all like to think it's cultural variety or stunning scenery that's top of our list of things we look for in a new place. But who are we kidding? If you're going for the full socio-cultural-anthropological analysis here, what really floats the traveller's boat, what we all really, truly place above all other things in the priorities stakes is... the grub and the bogs.

Think about it. You could be visiting the Great Wall of China or the Taj Mahal or the Niagara Falls, but if you're desperate for the loo, or your stomach's emitting those embarrassing growling noises it makes when it's empty, you're not going to be admiring the view. Instead of thinking 'Isn't it amazing this is the only man-made structure you can see from space', you're going to be thinking 'where's the nearest khazi?' or 'I could murder a chicken tikka massala'.

Unless your basic needs are catered for, it's hard to get truly inspired by even the grandest of landscapes or most historic of buildings. Home comforts are not called, well, home comforts for nothing. They're the things you most miss when you're away from home.

GRUB

Take food for example. Everyone sets off on their travels with the greatest anticipation of eating real, authentic foreign food, in real authentic foreign locations. And for a while it's exactly the way you dreamed it would be – delicate raw fish in Japan, fragrant coconut curries in Malaysia, rice and more rice in China. Every email you send home is full of the new taste sensations: 'I ate a locust!', 'The village elders cooked me a goat's head! With its eyes still in it!' Every exotic dish you taste adds to your smug feeling of having got away, of being finally, irrefutably Somewhere Different.

Rhys Ingram got a real flavour of Brazil after deciding to taste everything on offer (gapyear.com):

> Got my first taste of Acai which is lush! It's a purple fruit and they blend it and freeze it to make like a sorbet, put a bit of granola on top and you're away! On my way to go get some more in a minute as it was sooooooo good! Really filling too. The next day we went to a local market, had lunch with another family and went to see an indigenous village, which was cool. The villagers were preparing for a wedding so were busy building huts and things, though they took time out to give us tribal tattoos with a fruit. They only last a couple of weeks but it's all good fun. They'd also just finished cooking some alligator so let us try it – tasted pretty good I have to say! Then we went to make camp as we were staying on our own that night. We set up some logs in the trees, cut up fire wood, made it

waterproof where we would sleep and started to cook our food. Somehow it all worked out and we ate our chicken in the leaf plates we'd made.

But there comes a moment in every traveller's life when deep-fried spider just doesn't do it any more. Suddenly you don't care if you never see another chilli or taste another crab so fresh it practically nips your tonsils with its pincers on the way down. Usually it's a day when you're feeling particularly low, or vulnerable. Or, as in Stef Marianski's case, when you've made a particularly poor culinary choice at Shanghai's equivalent of the local greasy spoon (gapyear.com): 'I ate raw duck today! Did a lottery on the menu in this gaff and got raw shrimps followed by duck. And to make matters worse we were the only people in there, so eight waitresses gathered round watching us wrestle with the chopsticks!'

Maybe it's because it's your mum's birthday. Maybe it's because you've fallen out with your travelling companion after she cheated at hangman (since when do you draw hands AND fingers?). Maybe it's just because you're thousands of miles from home and you'd like, just for once, to go into a supermarket and not be stared and pointed at like an exhibit in a living museum installation. Whatever the reason you're feeling not quite tip top, you're going to find yourself sooner or later thinking of food. And what you'll be thinking is this: chips.

Okay, so not everyone will be thinking of chips, but it's a pretty good guess isn't it, and anyway, you know what I mean. Comfort food. For intrepid gapper Joe Bloomfield, his personal nutrition nadir came in Melaka, Malaysia (gapyear.com):

In between visiting museums, yesterday was spent quite shamefully eating comfort food. We fed the respective global beasts of Pizza Hut, KFC and McDonald's in one day. I know. It's wrong. I'm sorry, but when you've scoured the stalls looking for something to eat other than chicken feet, fried curry fish heads or intestine soup (with accompanying glossy photos) and seen a deep-fried duck, with beak still attached, hanging in front of you, you tend to crave the plasticky Western option occasionally. Better the devil you know and all that.

Occasionally though, being abroad will provide you with an unlooked-for nutritional nirvana – that rare moment where you combine the old with the new, the comforts of home with the exoticism of the alien. Like fast food, Russian stylee. Here's Stef Marianski (gapyear.com):

Number ten on my list of great things about Russia has gotta be the fast food. It's not fast food like England where you get a shrink-wrapped Big Mac or anything like that. In this one place you walk in and take a bowl and go to the food counter. You cram as much of whatever raw meat you prefer as you can get in the bowl and take it to the cooks who fry it in front of you. Legendary stuff! Also costs bugger all.

BOGS

What goes in must come out, as they say. And once you've eaten your raw meat, sipped your sake, slurped your freshly caught oysters and taken a big gulp of that curry they promised was mild and tried to see the funny side as your insides developed third-degree burns in a Mexican wave formation, your mind might well turn to the topic of personal hygiene facilities. In other words, you'll be thinking about the crapper. By the time globetrotting gapper Joe Bloomfield hit Malaysia, he had his priorities well and truly sorted, as he writes in his gapyear.com diary:

> Selamat Datang to my diary. That means 'welcome' by the way, two of the only words I know in the Malaysian language. The others are Keluar (exit) and Restoran (restaurant). I still don't know the word for toilet, which is probably unwise, considering I will probably need to know it quite urgently soon, judging by what they sell in some of the food stalls. We've now been in Malaysia for a couple of days after leaving Singapore on Tuesday. In case you're wondering, no, I haven't been holding it in for two days due to not knowing the word for toilet, I have in fact been looking at the pictures and following the one of the chap in the trousers.

THE TOILET LEAGUE

Stewart Ferris became something of a toilet connoisseur while researching his inter-railing bestseller *Don't Lean Out of the Window* (Summersdale). Here he shares the benefit of his considerable knowledge:

Always judge a nation by the quality of its public toilets. The more civilised the country, the more comfortable its conveniences. There are three leagues that a country can fit into:

1. **Fully civilised, e.g. Holland, with proper loos, soft tissue paper and running water.**

2. Lacking privacy, e.g. UK, with automatic doors that open and expose you to the world whether you're finished or not, and USA, where the cubicle doors start two feet from the floor and stop below eye level.

3. Downright weird, e.g. Germany, with toilets that provide an above-water platform to enable stool inspection.

   NB France, of course, doesn't enter the league at any level, as it is the only nation on earth that expects people to relieve themselves on a shower tray.

There can be few more burning issues to the average traveller than where, when and how he is to evacuate his bowels. Indeed, it can sometimes border on an obsession. Even the mildest case of Montezuma's revenge is enough to fill one with nostalgia for the toilet under the stairs at Mum and Dad's where one could retire post-breakfast with a cup of tea and a copy of the *Guardian*, and not have to reappear either until lunch or until someone needs the Packamac hanging on the back of the door.

I don't wish to appear uncharitable or, worse, guilty of sanitation snobbery, but a hole in the ground in someone's back yard surrounded by a grubby curtain and several scabby chickens just isn't the same thing, as Lindsay Bennett discovered in Tanzania (gapyear.com):

Thighs of steel?
Two words:
'squat toilet'
Need I say more?!

TRAVELLER'S TIPS

Gapper Edie Sanderson says pack some bog roll:

If strapped for space in the rucksack and weighing up the respective merits of that pair of gorgeous sparkly flip-flops or a bog roll, take the bog roll every time. If you take the cardboard tube out of the middle, it squishes down really small and, let's face it girls, doing the drip-dry thing is all very well for Number One's, but when you're talking Number Two's... I don't think I need say more.

Women have a particularly bad time of it. Not only do we have the two usual suspects to dispose of, for a few days every month they're joined by other pleasant items which also need to be found homes for – not always as easy as it sounds, as Liz Ely discovered when she arrived in India (gapyear.com).

We flew into Hyderabad, all ten of us project trust volunteers, where we were met by Bharavi, our representative, and his son Abilash with a camera in hand (so obviously some GORGEOUS photos of me emerging from customs with two heavy rucksacks after a twenty-four-hour journey).

I had my first feelings of culture shock and complete disorientation before I had even left the airport! My period started on one of the flights (I also had the worst period pain of my entire life – while all the other volunteers were excitedly peering out of the windows at Dubai I was hunched over wondering if the air hostesses carried morphine).

So obviously by Hyderabad I had a rather lovely item to dispose of. I found the toilets (I had very low expectations of Indian toilets but these managed to be more dire than I had ever envisaged) and I managed to wrap it in a few wet wipes, but there was no bin. Tired, I wandered around the toilets – do I flush? Do I put it in a little plastic bag and carry it around to a more convenient disposal point (what could be more convenient than a toilet!)? More to the point, do I have a plastic bag? Then a woman starts following me around and points to a (very well hidden) bin – then she points to the sink, I wash my hands, she points to the hand dryer – I use it. Then she starts saying something like 'maa' – I assume she is saying 'mam' so I say 'thank you' and walk out. Only later did I realise that she wanted money; I had just assumed she was a toilet attendant or something.

For some people, even trickier than the style of the loo, or where to put the things that should sensibly go down a loo but can't because you'd flood an entire town, is the vexing question of how to go to use a loo in the complete absence of anything resembling toilet paper. Here's Liz Ely again:

Had a few days of chilling out and wondering how to shower with a bucket and how exactly the left hand splashy splashy method of self-cleansing (post defecation) actually works (NB You have to TOUCH your own poo!).

Of course, the touching of the poo scenario then leads on to all manner of potential Toilet Etiquette blunders, as Joe Bloomfield found (gapyear.com):

We spent about two hours walking round in the sweltering heat and didn't get out of Little India. We ended up stopping at a strange little Indian fast-food place for some food, very much like the Indian version of Wimpy, and ordered a meal combo. We didn't have a clue what it was, but ended up munching it down with both hands. After I'd finished I read the advert sheet you get on the tray (just like in McDonald's) and realised I'd eaten my dessert by dipping it in curry sauce, and done so with my left hand. Anyone more familiar with the culture than I was will realise that eating with your left hand is a tremendous faux pas. You're supposed to reserve your left hand entirely for Andrex duties, hence using it to put food in your mouth is considered a little dirty.

WHY TOILETS MEAN SO MUCH TO TRAVELLERS

If there's one man who knows an awful lot about Toilets Around the Globe, it's Peter Moore, intrepid traveller and author of cult travel guide *No Shitting in the Toilet* (Bantam). Here he explains to potential gappers exactly why the humble WC takes on such major significance when you're on the road...

One of the first things you'll notice once you've hit the road is that travellers are obsessed with toilets. Put a group of travellers together and within five minutes they'll be talking bowel movements. (Having released a book called *No Shitting in the Toilet*, I guess I can't talk. But in my defence, it was named after a sign at Jack's Cafe in Dali in China. Really.)

My point, however, is that if you spend any time travelling, you can't help but be obsessed with all things scatological. A change in diet assures that you'll spend a lot more time on the John than you normally would back home. And toilets are the clearest indication that you're not in Kansas anymore (or Blackpool, for that matter).

The first time you gaze upon on a hole-in-the-ground Asian toilet will fundamentally change the way you look at the world. More than the funny tasting food, more than the strange costumes, more than the incomprehensible language. It rams home the point that people in other parts of the world do things a little differently. And if you've got a dose of Bali belly, it means you've got to learn how to do things a little differently too. And in a hurry.

At least Asian toilets are pretty easy to operate. There's a hole in the ground, and well, that's about it. Western-toilet style toilets are a different matter. I have yet to find two that work the same. Some have buttons, some have levers, some have chains. In fact, the only thing they all have in common is that in backpacker hostels they never ever work properly. (Now I don't want to appear culturally biased here. The first sighting of a Western sit-down style toilet by a Japanese tourist must be just as scary – the Australian hospitality industry is awash with apocryphal stories of footprints on the toilet seat.)

Even the humble choice of lavatorial reading material can give you the kind of cultural insight that watching the Discovery Channel never will. I stayed in a place in Albania where the guy had plastered the walls with the Book of Mormon and Penthouse Forum to help him expand his English vocabulary. On one wall, Jehoshaphat was telling the Mormons to come out of the desert. On the other, J.L. from Ohio was relating a tale that involved a brunette and a carrot.

As my old man was always fond of saying, it would be a funny old world if everyone was the same. But I tell you what. When your stomach is gurgling like a geyser at Rotarua and your bowels doing more twists than the US synchronised swimming team, you'll wish they were.

Chapter 8
WORKING ABROAD

'You grow up, you work half a century, you get a golden handshake, you rest a couple of years and you're dead. And the only thing that makes that crazy ride worthwhile is "Did I enjoy it?"'
David Brent, The Office

Hands up who can guess the number one gripe about gap years from people who've never taken one? Yes, in first position comes the old favourite: 'Just an excuse for a bloody long holiday, isn't it?' And let's face it, there's more than a grain of truth in that (but then, how many of the 'two-weeks-in-Majorca-each-year' brigade who tend to lodge this complaint would actually say no to an eight-month foreign adventure? That'd be not many, then).

Yet, contrary to all stereotypes, there are many gappers who can't consider a gap year without that most offensive of all four-letter words springing to mind: work. For some it's an altruistic calling, for others a financial imperative, and for the rest it's a chance to have something impressive to add to an otherwise lacklustre CV.

Working abroad fantasies usually fall into one of two categories.

CATEGORY ONE: THE INGRID BERGMAN FANTASY

There's an old Ingrid Bergman film, *The Inn of the Sixth Happiness*, where she plays a British woman who runs an orphanage in China. When war breaks out, instead of abandoning them to their fate, she selflessly rounds up all the children, plonks one of those pointy straw hats on her head and walks for days over perilous mountain ranges, dodging bullets and enemy roadblocks until they get to safety and a hero's welcome. Well, if we're being completely honest, most of us harbour secret Ingrid Bergman aspirations. We dream of going off to some needy part of the world and doing something self-sacrificing that will really Make a Difference. We want to feel like we're putting something back (and if we get a little personal buzz of satisfaction out of it, so much the better).

CATEGORY TWO: THE ANNA WINTOUR FANTASY

This is the one where you get a job abroad, take the place by storm, and are immediately elevated to the position of Editor of New York *Vogue** (* substitute whichever country and/or iconic job takes your imagination). Whereupon you become a toast-of-the-town honorary New Yorker (or Barcelonian, Hong Konger, etc.), totally at home and comfortable and feted in your adopted culture. And you get to wear loads of nice clothes and be very thin and… sorry, carried away by that one.

Whatever variation of these two themes your working abroad fantasy involves, you can be sure of one thing. The reality will be completely and utterly different.

VOLUNTEERING

The big thing to remember about volunteering is you probably won't get to directly save any lives, invent ways of bringing water to drought-ridden villages or single-handedly save a species from extinction. However, even if you downsize your expectations, you can still make a huge difference. Sir Hugh Pike, Associate of GAP Activity Projects, says:

> Travel for its own sake is fine, as far as it goes. And there's nothing wrong with having fun. GAP offers both of these in abundance, but they are the result, not the cause. The cause is to live and work among people of a different culture, outlook and way of life from your own; and to seek fulfilment and personal development through volunteering to help others and by undertaking a serious job of work.

James Chapman of gap year organisers Outreach International explains that it pays to examine your own motivation before deciding to become a volunteer.

> Some people think they want to do an outreach project but when I meet them, they're not right. They genuinely think that, at eighteen, they're going to be saving the world. You have to be realistic and we have to be careful. Sometimes people want to go on the projects in Mexico because they think it's a party place. But it's no good to rock up in the morning hung over when you're dealing with vulnerable children.
>
> But having said that, volunteers often mature enormously as individuals during their placement. Parents commonly say, 'We sent a little girl and she came back a woman.'
>
> You get to master a new language and feel like you've done something to help the world. I saw a young

girl the other day who'd been on a placement working with street children in Ecuador. I asked, 'How was it?' She said, 'I didn't get to do all the big things I'd expected but what I did manage to do was to bring a smile to a child's face every day.' Because street children don't smile. They don't have anything to smile about. But she made them smile every day for ninety days and she'll remember that for the rest of her life.

WORKING ABROAD WITH VSO

Voluntary Services Overseas is one of the world's oldest international development charities that works through volunteers. The Youth for Development scheme sends people who already have a year's worth of experience in community or voluntary work to undertake projects in areas like IT, peer education around HIV and AIDS, health, fundraising, environmental education and disability rights. The six-month Global Xchange programme teams British-based volunteers with the same number from a developing country, who collaborate on community initiatives in the UK and then abroad. VSO provide accommodation, flights, medical and travel insurance, visas, permits, training and a living allowance. In return volunteers are asked to fundraise between £600 and £900. Abbie Fulbook from VSO says, 'Fundraising is all about asking people for support – if you don't ask you don't get – and people are generally more than happy to help if you mention a well-known charity like VSO. Keep your fundraising simple, if you're already having a birthday party, why not use it as a fundraising opportunity? Be persistent and don't forget to enjoy yourself!'

As I mentioned in Chapter 1, there have been recent rumblings of discontent about just how useful some gap year projects are to the communities they're aiming to serve. And whether, indeed, they can sometimes be counter-constructive – using up valuable local resources or leaving needy groups in the lurch when a placement ends. That's why it's vital to ask questions about your placement such as whether it has the support of the local community, whether the organisation employs local staff, what percentage of your fee will go directly to the programme and whether you'll be replaced by another volunteer when you leave.

Usually you'll get some sort of training for a volunteer placement. But be aware – there are scenarios that no amount of training can quite prepare you for, as gapyear.com's Chris Bowden discovered on his teaching placement in Kenya.

> What do you find on top of Mount Kenya that you do not find anywhere else in Kenya? Blank faces from the kids. I drew _ _ _ _ on the board and put the first 's' and last 'w' letters in for them. Blank faces. Filled in the rest to create the word 'snow' and was again greeted by blank faces. None of them had ever seen or heard of snow! I'm still trying to explain it to them now!

Some volunteers are initially dismayed to find that the work they're expected to do is less about building bridges between cultures and more about building public conveniences and sewage systems. Lisa Hargreaves still smiles when she remembers detouring to Sri Lanka during her gap year round-the-world trip to help with the tsunami rebuilding effort and being assigned to clearing up rubbish duties. She recalls:

I had this vision of swanning about tending the sick and needy or looking after abandoned babies. Instead I was picking up old shoes and bits of broken wood. But you know, each of those old shoes had a story to tell, and it's incredible how quickly you forget your own silly vanity in the face of so much destruction.

James Chapman from Outreach International calls it 'stepping out of your own comfort zone' and there's little doubt that volunteering to do something completely different to benefit other people can be a hugely rewarding experience, as Amy Lambert found when she worked in a medical centre in Cambodia helping people injured by land mines rebuild their lives. She recounts in her gapyear.com diary:

> We went to another centre where we'll be teaching, where they train amputees in professions like hairdressing, bike repairs and agriculture, then give them loans to set up a business back in their community, which was amazing!
>
> There was one old man at the rehabilitation centre this week who'd had a stroke in August and couldn't get out of bed since. They brought him to the centre and gave him a wheelchair and helped him to walk again with a frame. It was so amazing – he just looked so happy! I have never seen anyone look so grateful and happy in my life – hopefully we'll see a lot more of that!
>
> We've had a lot more patients in, one who we've nicknamed George (because we can't pronounce his real name, even after a week of being told about ten times a day). He lost his leg in a land-mine accident and his old prosthesis has rubbed huge sores on his stump.

So he's at the centre for a few weeks while his leg heals and they make him a new prosthetic leg. When he first arrived he looked a little scared of us, but he's actually a really good laugh now he's coming out of himself. We've been playing wheelchair basketball, sitting-down badminton (until George gets his new leg) and we even taught him to play snap, although I'm still not sure he really gets it!

Many gappers love the idea of volunteering to 'put something back' but simply don't think they have it in them to work in what can be extremely emotionally distressing circumstances, such as dealing with land-mine victims or street children. Some feel a sense of shame about admitting it, but it's better to voice your doubts or limitations up front and find something else worthwhile to do rather than giving up on the whole idea of volunteering and spending your gap year working in a call centre in Croydon instead. There's loads of stuff you can do that doesn't put you on the frontline of human suffering. Such as working on an organic farm in Costa Rica, like Rachael Hodnett (gapyear.com):

The farm is beautiful, there are about eight to ten volunteers at any one time and we all live in Casa Ylang Ylang which is a very pretty, very airy house, only about a year old. The farm is an organic farm and they also practise biodynamics, which I have to say I am a bit sceptical about. Things like adding special substances (minerals from rocks, cow dung, etc.) to a bucket of water and stirring it for an hour to create a vortex that takes bad energies out of the air and then you spray it onto the crops/soil. Sometimes once you have done that it rains within forty-eight hours. I'm sure someone else could explain it far better than me. It seems to work, though!

We work four hours a day, five days a week, from 6 30 am till 10 30 am. We do all sorts of work – transplanting passion fruit plants and lettuces, seeding, clearing up in general, weeding the ponds. They had four of us girls weeding the big duck pond the other day, with the water up to our shoulders – quite refreshing as it's so humid here, but a bit smelly!

Sometimes volunteer work allows you to get the feel-good factor of knowing you're helping out, alongside the rather less altruistic knowledge that you're notching up a few Brownie points when it comes to future careers. Gapyear.com's Sarah Ford went on a volunteer placement to Ghana that was part teaching and part journalism – here's her diary entry from her first month as a newspaper photographer.

I've finally started at the *Daily Dispatch*. Went out a couple of weeks ago and took photos of some street children, those having to sell things to survive, for a story on child trafficking. It was pretty amazing since I got to see parts of Accra that I probably would never have seen. We went to this big food market. I've walked past the entrance before but never knew it was even there really. Pretty extraordinary as it was so crowded, so hot and very smelly. Plus I got photos I would never have been able to get otherwise. Some people are pretty funny about you taking their photograph – some refused, some took a lot of persuading. I had a Ghanaian woman with me which made it easier. Still pretty frustrating as I must have missed a lot of great photos as I couldn't just be spontaneous.

Saw a sports programme being filmed, and got to sit in the studio as the presenter is the editor of the sports paper I'm working for. That's a cool thing about Ghana, you do things you never thought you would get the opportunity to do otherwise.

YOU'RE THERE TO HELP, NOT CONVERT

The great thing about being Somewhere Completely Different is that they do everything Completely Differently. It can come as a shock to some gappers on voluntary placements to realise that this might include attitudes and behaviour that we consider old-fashioned, barbaric or just frustratingly inept. The thing to remember, and it can be a hard one for someone arriving with a missionary zeal to make everything better, is that you're there to adapt to their culture – not to make them adapt to yours. Sarah Ford found it hard to witness how children were treated in the Ghanaian orphanage she was photographing, as she describes in her gapyear.com diary:

I was in the room with the young children, mainly aged one to three but there was a five-month-old baby as well. There were about forty children in a room that was small for the number of children. There were no toys, colouring crayons or games. I arrived just as they were singing with the children and that's the only kind of activity I saw, though they might have done more before I arrived. There were alphabet paintings on the wall. I kept on thinking about work back home and the nursery which isn't the best equipped but compared to the place in Ghana is amazing. They play and they're happy and I know material possessions aren't everything but I really think books and jigsaws and some toys would just be so much more stimulating for them. The children there are caned, and threatened a lot. The thing I really didn't like was when one girl had a toilet-related accident and the teacher stood her up in front of the other children and shouted sh-sh-sh-sh and then the other children joined in with shaming her. It was pretty humiliating.

Even the teaching side of Sarah Ford's placement caused her some internal conflict:

So far, what I've noticed about the education here is that they tend to do things in a kind of parrot fashion – repeating things, copying lots off the board. I remember my primary school where there were a lot more things like projects and working in groups – being creative and expressing opinions. I think, so far, I probably prefer the English version.

For Harriet Chambers, teaching English at a university in Ho Chi Minh City similarly failed to be the inspiring experience she'd hoped for (gapyear.com):

We've started teaching at a university which has its good moments and its bad. Some of the classes are great and so are some of the staff, but others just won't respond to anything you say, however hard you try. We were warned that Vietnamese students were very passive and shy but I really wasn't expecting it at this level. However, the one major problem is that the English teachers don't appear to speak English! I had one today who walked into my class, cigarette in one hand, lunch in the other, and proceeded to talk to the class in Vietnamese – now that's fine, I understand that Vietnamese people tend to speak Vietnamese, but last time I checked he was meant to be teaching them English! As for the rest of the university, they've given us timetables and told us to follow them but they are wrong and so for the last three days we haven't made it to one lesson at the right time, or even to the right lesson for that matter. I guess it's just the way things work here, laid back and yet chaotic at the same time – half the students don't even turn up until twenty minutes into the lesson. And the lecturers don't seem to care – they just wander in and sit down!

ODD-JOBBING

What do you do if you want to travel, but only have enough cash to get you halfway to where you want to go? Easy answer – you get a job while abroad. What could be better? That way you get to really experience a different culture while earning dosh at the same time. Result! Ryan Price, who has been working in Australia with his partner, Cy, believes it's definitely the way to go.

Working adds a new perspective to your trip because you get to 'live' somewhere. Plus you can extend your trip by earning some funds! As UK and French citizens we have both been able to get one-year work/travel visas for Australia and New Zealand. You have to be eighteen to thirty, without children, have health insurance and proof of funds. I've found it easy to get work in Australia. I've been able to get plenty of HR work and done more general admin when the market has been quiet. Cy has worked in catering. You are limited to working for the same employer for a maximum of three months, which can limit opportunities. This is being increased to six months. If you spend at least three months working in rural Australia picking crops (and some other agricultural seasonal jobs) you can apply for a second year in Oz.

But many gappers are disappointed to discover that the roads of Sydney (or Auckland, Tokyo or wherever) are not lined with gold, or even copper (which everyone knows is so worthless nowadays, it's cheaper to leave a 2p coin on the ground than squander the nanosecond of potential earning time it would take to pick it up). Finding a job abroad is a lot harder than finding a job at home – and twice as frustrating. Here's Ali Potter's job-hunting diary (gapyear.com):

Arrggggh! You hear about all the opportunities in Oz but you get here and it's mission impossible to get a job and somewhere to stay! Even so I might have a job (fingers crossed) doing street promotions BUT I WILL NOT WEAR A CHICKEN SUIT, OKAY? I WILL NOT! The apartment thing is harder because Sydney swells with backpackers around this time of year.

Sydney seems to be a particularly difficult nut to crack when it comes to securing that perfect job... or just any job really. It could be because more British gappers go there than anywhere else in the whole universe so all the jobs have already been taken by people who had the foresight to get an earlier flight than you and are very smug about it, too. Or it could just be because jobs are hard to come by. But the fact is, it's all a bit of a bun fight. Here's Samantha Joly's experience, as reported in her gapyear.com diary.

The last time I left you I was off for a job interview, not actually knowing what the job was for. Wasn't that an experience? Basically, it turned out that the interview was putting me with a whole bunch of employees and sending me out with them to see if I was up to the job. Let me explain a normal day for these people. They get to the office in Sydney at about 12.30 pm, then they have a 'motivational meeting' for about an hour, they then receive their posts for the day and a map to get there. At around 2 pm they all board a train which takes them to their destination. This train journey lasts for at least an hour every day and there is next to no talking (they are all so tired from work the day before, even though they don't have to be at work until 12.30 pm!). Once they get to the place they've been allocated they then spend the next one and a half hours eating (again, hardly any talking, they were a rather sullen bunch). Only then did I actually find out what it was that their job consisted of. Instead of accosting people on the street (which I had originally thought the job was), they actually knock on people's doors! Argh!

Basically, I couldn't get out of there quick enough – standing on the street I could just about have managed, but actually invading people's homes and trying to shame them into signing up to some charity I won't ever do. So I just left them (still eating) and got the train back home! They have to pay for their transport and food and only get paid by commission – and you can imagine how many people will actually sign up to these things – so there is a very high chance that they end up with nothing at all!

Then there was more job hunting. Well, that didn't go exactly to plan really... After everything that people told me about how easy it would be to get a job in Sydney... Pah! They know nothing! I spent about a week just wandering around handing my CV in to bars and pubs with almost every one of them saying something along the lines of, 'Oh, we've only just hired someone, you should have come last week'. Grrrrrrr! So, I've decided finally to just give up job hunting and worry about the money when I get home – dangerous, some might say...

TRAVELLER'S TOP TIP

Keep your cool, says Karen Golightly:

Working abroad is rarely as glamorous as you might think. This is where the real culture shock comes in. Be prepared to do things differently and don't show your frustration if the working culture is less effective. Make suggestions if you think they'll work – but losing your temper will just make you look stupid and arrogant.

Even if you are lucky enough to find a job, it rarely lives up to the Anna Wintour fantasy scenario. In fact, it's not likely to live up to any kind of fantasy scenario – or else some other qualified American, Australian, German, Fijian would have come along and taken it themselves, now, wouldn't they? Ewan Dinwiddie learned this the hard way when he tried to make a little fast cash Down Under (gapyear.com):

And so to Melbourne where I find myself now. With my funds running dangerously low I was relieved to hear that there was some work going that actually started the same day. Now, you may think that working as an elf-type person at Santa's Kingdom I couldn't really sink any lower, but I may have achieved it here. Carnival was in town so… for four days I was a carnie! I was working on a toss-the-ball-in-the-bucket scam, er… I mean game. It was very nearly impossible to win – we had maybe one winner out of every few hundred punters. And considering they were paying five bucks a go for a cuddly toy imported from China for thirty cents it was almost criminally scandalous. I wasn't too fussed about taking away hard-earned cash from forty-year-old blokes (who should have caught on by now, anyway) but I can't say I enjoyed relieving small kids of their week's pocket money to play a game they had sod all chance of winning. My carnie boss didn't seem to have the same moral problems, however, and you could almost see his face light up when a bunch of gullible nippers approached!

Not only was I working as a carnie, but I was also living as one. Myself and another English lad didn't see the point in paying twenty-odd bucks a night to sleep in a hostel and so, with the permission of our carnie boss, decided to kip behind our stall for three nights! I had some surprisingly good nights' sleep. Our alarm clock was the huge generator that began roaring away at eight each morning.

Sometimes the jobs you think will be the most deadly boring actually turn out to be surprisingly okay – and vice versa. Even fruit picking in the rain can have its own rewards, as Heather Fitsell reports in her gapyear.com diary:

I came across an employment agency in Perth and through them I have ended up in the small town of Manjimup in the southwest, picking apples. The picking is tiring, but much better than the three weeks I spent at the construction company before I left Sydney! I'm outdoors for a start, trying to improve the colour of my skin through the aid of SPF30 suncream! It is much colder down here than up in Perth and we have had rain believe it or not! I got soaked right through one day and took the next day off due to my lack of wet weather gear which has now been purchased!

Chapter 9
LONG JOURNEYS

'The journey not the arrival matters.'
T S Eliot

Here's a quick test to keep you on your toes. Study the two following journey scenarios:

JOURNEY SCENARIO ONE

It's dusk. You're sitting atop an old Landrover, rattling along a dusty African road with your trusty rucksack by your side. As the sun sets like a blood orange in the sky behind you, one of your fellow travellers gets out an old guitar and plays softly as you all pass around a miraculously ice-cold beer and swap intimate, fascinating travel tales long into the night.

JOURNEY SCENARIO TWO

It's two o'clock on a blazing South American afternoon and you're sitting in a packed bus, squished between a large, sweaty man with halitosis and a woman with a live chicken on her lap. You're dying of thirst, but you dare not let any refreshment pass your lips because your insides are still protesting in the only way they know how about that dodgy kebab you got at the last-but-one toilet stop. Still, just another twenty-three hours to go. No worries. Just as long as that baby in front of you doesn't do another one of its projectile vomitting party tricks... Oh, spoke too soon. Well, at least you hadn't bothered to change your T-shirt since the last time, and orange is such a forgiving colour...

TRAVELLER'S TOP TIP

Trust your instincts, advises Karen Golightly:

I was once left behind at a rest stop by a bus going to Malaysia from Thailand. Luckily a local fella at the stop (loosely linked with the bus company) was there and told me to jump in the back of his pick-up and we raced to catch up with the bus. Took about thirty minutes (and I'd only missed it by ten minutes by going to the loo). After ten minutes I was beginning to think I'd end up in a ditch by a deserted farmhouse, so I made sure I had my penknife in my pocket, just in case, and started trying to get my bearings by the sun (how ridiculous – just goes to show what panic does). Turns out he was a sound fella and I got my bus okay, but it was slightly stupid of me in hindsight. However, this does raise another point, that you should always trust your instincts. Judge the risk: are you capable of getting out of a tricky situation? Even if the answer is yes, if your instinct says 'no', don't do it!

Okay, now answer the following question: which scenario is more 'real'?

The answer is – as you've probably guessed by now, because what's the point of including questions unless they're trick ones – they both are! Over the course of your gap year you're likely to have great journeys, dreadful journeys, journeys where you think you might spontaneously combust if you see another travel backgammon set and journeys where you're so chilled you don't even want to get off at the end.

You're going to have journeys you've planned for months, and journeys you've undertaken on a complete whim. You'll have journeys with people you like lots and journeys with people you'd like to poke in the eye with a sharp stick rather than have to listen to them repeating the same old stories about their whacky travel adventures (why is it that drinking a bucket of tequila and falling asleep with one's head down a toilet never fails to amuse some people?).

Even if you plan on spending a big chunk of your gap year in one place, travelling is still likely to feature large on your 'things to do' list. And this is travel unlike anything you've ever known. It's not the same as getting the National Express from Victoria Bus Station to Liverpool, nor does it in any way resemble jumping on a train in Brighton and getting off in, well, somewhere else entirely. Unless you make a habit of pointlessly circumnavigating the country making good use of its splendid coach/rail transport links, you're going to be hard pressed to spend more than a few hours on any journey in Britain (of course, I'm not including delays, strikes or the wrong kind of leaves on the track in this equation).

Travelling abroad, on the other hand, is a whole different thing. For a start, once you're no longer on an island the size of a lentil you can make journeys that start in one country and end up three countries along. You can make journeys in rickety buses, journeys in sleeper trains, journeys by raft, by rickshaw and by rhino (well, okay, probably unlikely, but it does begin with 'r'). Suddenly the journey isn't just a way of getting Somewhere, it's the very Somewhere you wanted to be in the first place.

Now settled in a farmhouse in France, writer Emily Barr still remembers with great fondness her travelling days...

> I look back now on the long, boring journeys with a great feeling of nostalgia. My main advice would be to enjoy them! In fact, when I think back to my travelling year, I picture myself on a massively overloaded bus in Asia, squashed in between a woman with five chickens on her lap and a man with a goat asleep on his feet. And there I am in the middle, reading a novel. Every time the bus stops, hands appear through the windows offering food and drink for sale. The road is potholed, the heat almost unbearable, and there is absolutely nothing you can do but wait it out.

TRAVELLER'S TOP TIP

Stewart Ferris, author of inter-railing memoirs *Don't Lean Out of the Window* and *Don't Mention the War*, gives this handy advice for coping with long, boring journeys: 'Once you've learned all the swear words of the country you're going to, try passing the time by counting exotic moustaches, unsafe-looking buildings and bad drivers.'

The key to enjoying travelling abroad is to remember all the things you'd expect from a passenger's charter back home – Efficient service! Attentive staff! Clean toilets! Buses with the requisite number of wheels! – and accept that here they don't mean anything at all (unless of course you're travelling in Germany or Scandinavia or Japan where the rule is to remember everything you'd expect from a passenger's charter back home and then multiply to the power of ten, although possibly not the number of bus wheels, or you'd run out of undercarriage space). Once you free yourself from expectations, you can sit back and enjoy all the detours, mishaps and downright surreal experiences that come your way. Dhruti Shah, who spent three months backpacking around Thailand, Laos, Cambodia and Vietnam, remembers doing just that on an interminable trans-Asian bus journey.

We tended to travel overland by coach and bus. One of the longest journeys we had to take was between Vientiane, Laos and Hanoi, Vietnam. It took us twenty-seven hours and was an interesting ride to say the least. Not only did we have to cope with having to give bribes to the border control, but at one point the coach stopped in the middle of nowhere and all of the Vietnamese travellers jumped off and stayed in a hotel. We had to wait on a freezing cold bus, uncertain about what on earth was going on. Then, when we got into Vietnam, our bus got hit by a truck, before proceeding to run over a dog. When travelling you've got to take things like this in your stride.

TRAVELLER'S TOP TIP
'Don't Panic!' says James Whitaker...

Reliability is not often a feature of the type of travel networks travellers use (any more than it is in

England, but it always seems more serious when you're in unfamiliar surroundings). This is rarely a real problem, as long as you remember that it is really not desperately serious. Travelling on a rather rickety bus through Malaysia, we broke down (which seems to be an obligatory occurrence during most long-distance journeys) and our initial reaction was one of slight panic mixed with utter helplessness, particularly as there were no English speakers in sight. Provided you have no urgent appointments at your destination, it is never as serious as it first seems. Reason it out: you're not simply going to be left there; someone will be by to collect you or fix the bus or train before long.

Former gapper Jane Yettram developed a three-point Talk–Look–Read approach to get her through the long, boring journeys she took with her (now) husband on their long-distant gap year.

1. Talk to people – and not just other Westerners. Even though I know zilch about cricket, I have discussed spin-bowling with mad keen Indian cricket fans on forty-hour train journeys, and chatted to Indian holidaymakers in the Himalayas. One guy we met now visits us frequently in London. And another has children our kids' ages, and we hope to take the children over to meet them soon. We also made long-term friendships with other travellers.

2. Remember that although journeys can be long and boring, gazing out of the window at wallowing water buffalo,

emerald rice paddies and even teeming cities is fascinating compared to taking the 7.46 to Waterloo.

3. Primarily, I just read – swapping books at various stalls or with other travellers along the way. The swap bookshop in Dharamsala is one of the best bookshops I've ever been to!

JOURNEYS FROM HELL: ONE

This account is from Terry McDermott, travelling in Bolivia.

The morning started very early with our leaving the Isla del Sol on Lake Titicaca, the highest navigable lake in the world. The boat was loaded up to sinking point with a selection of native ladies, backpackers and sacks of rice, resulting in a circular motion to the vessel and shortly thereafter, my turning green and chucking my guts up into a bailing-out bucket.

After finally docking in Copacabana, the lake's main sea port, we discovered at the local bus office that the road to La Paz, Bolivia's capital, was blocked by protesters. If we stood any chance of getting there, we would have to go back into Peru and take another bus from a different border town to try another route.

A large group of foreigners including us set off. We arrived around 2 pm and realised that about every other person trying to get to La Paz had had the same idea – the small town was chock-full of lorries, camper vans, four-by-fours and buses, but nothing was moving – the road here was also blocked. After a while, however, a few vehicles did start to move and as I prided myself as being something of a Mr Fix-It among backpackers, I decided I would find us a vehicle out of the place.

I started on a young Bolivian family in a camper van and although initially enthusiastic, they for some reason got cold feet about taking us and eventually drove off despite my scribbling higher and higher offers in the dust on their windscreen. An old Blue Bird bus proved a better bet and after getting together about ten other backpackers willing to pay US$10 a head, we set off, not before collecting some twenty natives taking advantage of one of the few buses out of town. Note this was about 6 pm.

For an hour or so, there was little disturbance as we drove along a flat, straight, well-paved road. We had to stop a few times to clear the highway of some small rocks that had been put there by protesters but there was no sign of anyone. If this was what had closed a road, it was pretty pathetic!

We then stopped at another one of these roadblocks; it was by then about 7 pm and dark. All the boys got off and once again cleared the stones and mud from the road. Suddenly there was some commotion back at the bus. Some man had gone aboard and aggressively started asking if anyone was carrying any food – fish, cheese, meat, etc. The natives on the bus at his instruction started taking out packages containing various food stuffs and he angrily got off.

I looked out my window to see masked men emerging from the darkness. Suddenly the bus windows started smashing, one after another. We all threw our backpacks over ourselves and went into brace position! The smashing continued and when the bus tried to move, the tyres burst as the bandits had placed glass under them. Suddenly the police appeared armed with machine guns and the bandits fled. The entire windscreen was smashed, but the windows on my side of the bus were 'only' about 50% broken and some of those just had clear holes through them, so the entire window wasn't broken. On the other side, however, the windows were pretty much all broken.

The police escorted us back to a small town where we sat for a while as the driver and bus boy replaced the tyres. Some old hippy Chileans dressed in knitted hats decided the bus needed some relaxing so began wafting burning sage under all our noses – the Bolivians looked more frightened by this than anything else. I presumed we would be going back to the border; however, it turned out we were going to attempt the trip to La Paz via the 'old road'! So after two hours of repairs, replacing tyres, putting sticky tape on all the broken windows, we set off again.

At the entrance to the 'old road' we found more protesters but this lot were amenable to a bit of bribery so the driver paid them and we were allowed to pass. The 'old road' as it turned out was not on a flat plateau like the new road, but rather passed over a mountain – and it had just started to snow. So here we were at the bottom of a mountain, with many windows missing, already some 3,500 metres above sea level and climbing, with snow coming through all the holes in the bus. I had the only empty seat next to me and was joined by a young Mexican backpacker who had been sitting with his girlfriend next to one of the larger holes on the other side. Being the gentleman that he was, when the snow started, he had left his blustery corner to join me, leaving his poor girlfriend to freeze. Every now and then he would forlornly shout, 'Marie! Marie! Are you okay?' and she would chatter back, 'Si!' He would then turn around quite contented and offer me more of his peanut brittle bar.

Halfway up the mountain, we hit a traffic jam. All the buses on the way to La Paz were using this road and we were the very last bus in the queue. With the snow, no bus could make it up the meandering mountain road without lots of pushing. So all the boys had to dismount and push each bus along. This went on for four hours – starting at two in the morning. I began by staying on our bus since I was fat and didn't want to help, but as we skidded and slid up the road, I realised that there was significant danger of plummeting into the ravine at the side of the road, so I dismounted and helped push with my little finger.

By the time we got to the last bend at the top of the mountain, the only bus left was ours. We'd pushed the rest up the mountain and once at the summit, they'd sped away. That last corner was a killer, I can tell you – over 4,000 metres above sea level, around 5.30 in the morning, dark, exhausted! At the peak, the driver promptly turned off the engine and said we would have to wait until sunrise before starting the descent.

The misery of it! I remember sitting in my seat wrapped in a white cotton sheet, shivering, soaking from the snow and wanting to die.

At first light, we moved downwards and encountered a few more blockages, such as a bridge removed from over a river – we just drove through the river – and some holes in the road, but nothing capable of stopping the conquerors of the mountain!

The driver dropped us off at around midday some ten or so miles outside La Paz, in front of a cement factory, in a place resembling Chernobyl – we were delighted!

When you're dealing with journeys that take longer than a city mini-break, it's often tempting to turn to the kind of external help that comes either in a bottle of something with more proof than Hercule Poirot or a brown paper bag from a helpful pharmacist to help while away a few hours or even days. Travel journalist and BBC *Holiday* programme presenter Sankha Guha has had plenty of opportunities to perfect his Long Journey Survival Techniques:

My longest journey took forty-three hours – from Sydney to Rio via Fiji, Tahiti, LA, Lima and São Paulo. We crossed the international date line once, both tropics twice and the equator twice. I was so dazed and confused that I was beyond caring, beyond reality and beyond boredom. If you really can't deal with it you could try some kind of sleeping pill. Better still – get someone to pay for business class or blag yourself an upgrade. Drink lots of free champagne and annoy the bankers around you in any way possible.

JOURNEYS FROM HELL: TWO

In his gapyear.com diary, Neil Jones describes his travels in Peru:

And so at 3.30 am, setting off up the canyon on our hike out, I was feeling so bad, if I had come across a guy with a donkey I think I would have bought it off him. Oh, and this was my birthday, happy twenty-first and the hike from hell. This was the hardest thing I've ever done. I felt faint the whole time. And just wanted to keel over. But the important thing was to get to the top before the full heat of the sun was upon us. We made it with legs of lead, but my birthday was not over yet. I still had the fun local bus to enjoy.

My seat was right at the front, up against the driver's compartment. Even if you were under five foot tall you would have no leg room. So I had legs cramping up from the hike every five minutes, and added to this a bus filled to five times its capacity, with an old lady sitting on my legs, two kids on my lap, an old guy dripping ice cream on my head, and chicken feed falling on my head from the hole in the bag overhead. Oh, and three people leaning against me, and the woman next to me drooling on my shoulder. And feeling so ill that I should be in bed for month – all this while driving along the bumpiest road in Peru.

Emily Barr also opted for the 'Knock Yourself Out By Any Means Possible' method of travelling on more than one occasion, although in retrospect, she's not quite sure it was such a great idea…

Long journeys are the essence of travelling, and after a while you develop a nice zen attitude and may even get the hang of sleeping in the middle of the mayhem.

Having said that, in Thailand I went to a pharmacy and asked for something to help me sleep on an overnight train. I have no idea what he gave me, but whatever it was, it was good! As long as I felt I wasn't at any personal risk, I would take a magic pill on an overnight bus or train journey, and wake, refreshed, ten hours later. That was a godsend. I innocently carried my special pills over several Asian borders, which, with hindsight, was probably not a good idea as they were quite possibly illegal and could have landed me in an unimaginable amount of trouble.

JOURNEYS FROM HELL: THREE

Here's Amy Lambert's experience in Cambodia (gapyear.com):

We came back to Kratie on Sunday, via the worst bus journey ever. Don't sit at the back on a bus in Cambodia. You will be right over the wheels so you feel every bump and pot hole (and there are a lot!). You will also be right over the engine, which heats up to about 40 degrees. And to top it all off, the back seats have no air-con vents. To end that wonderful day, we got stuck out in the middle of a torrential rainstorm and got drenched running home. The only good thing to come out of it were the hilarious photos we got of us all looking like we'd been in the shower with our clothes on.

When we're talking about countries where drug use is still a hanging offence, nobody is seriously recommending Doping Up to the Eyeballs as a strategy for getting through tedious trips. However, if you're desperate for sleep, a mild sleeping pill from a friendly chemists can sometimes be a help – just make sure you're travelling with a friend you can trust to wake you up if a) you've arrived wherever you wanted to go, or b) the chicken next to you has been sick into your rucksack (note to self: check if chickens possess gagging reflex). One thing that would, of course, be a very, very silly thing to do on a long journey, is to drink yourself into oblivion. Here, dear Reader, is a cautionary tale on that very subject from reluctant flier Julian Draper:

I hate flying. As a result I tend to consume excessive amounts of spirits (neat) together with valium, the intoxicating union of which allows me to get on a plane, and upon taking one such flight from Honolulu to Vancouver I persuaded my travelling buddy to join me. The time in between having it out with a US airport official who wouldn't let me carry my cocktail on to the plane and landing is lost to memory. What most certainly isn't lost is Canadian immigration, which I had assumed would be a doddle.

The deadpan immigration guy began hitting us with a long line of questions: 'Are you here on holiday? Have you been to America? Are you British Citizens?' (Did he LOOK at our passports?) We realised that all we had to do was nod and say 'yes' to each banal question. Easy, and particularly welcome given the state we were in. That is, until he asked us if we'd recently taken any illegal substances. 'Yes,' we answered. The gravity of this response was beautifully brought home with a symbolically heavy red stamp pounded onto our passports. We were promptly marched off and had to stand in our underpants while several sniffer dogs pulled our bags to pieces. After a most thorough investigation, a woman, who had the look of someone who has just been magnificently thwarted, pulled a spoon out of my belongings in frustration. 'What's this?' she asked aggressively. Given our already weak and deteriorating state, our only response was to laugh and laugh until our knees gave way. At which point they let us go.

LOST IN TRANSITION

One of the biggest drags about travelling is having your luggage lost, as these gappers attest...

Pete Kehoe says, 'My lowest point by far was having my luggage left behind in Fiji! We left in 30-degree heat and when we arrived in San Fransisco it was 6 degrees! My only possessions were a T-shirt, a pair of thin trousers and my flip-flops!'

Joe Bloomfield's mate Andy failed to see the funny side when his bag went missing at baggage reclaim during a one-hour stopover in Brisbane (gapyear.com):

Things did not look good, so while I checked the other carousels Andy and Lewis went to the baggage reclaim desk and asked the vacant looking chap behind the counter if they had any bags round the back that hadn't come on yet. As I joined them after my fruitless search the guy was explaining that all the bags were up, and it was probably there but we'd missed it. He then took the little bar-coded baggage receipt and went to check the number against the tags on the few remaining bags to see if we'd had a sudden attack of 'Thick', forgotten what Andy's luggage looked like and had been watching it repeatedly pass us on the conveyor belt without realising it was his.

While this tie-wearing shaved monkey was off wasting precious minutes busying himself with his little errand we asked his supervisor (who seemed to have a bit more brains and sense of urgency) what to do. He told us that we should get on our connection, fill out a report at Cairns and get it sorted from there.

Andy at this point had a face like thunder. We have a nickname for him when he gets in a mood, namely 'Mummra', due to his personality traits similar to those of the baddy in Thundercats. This was a definite Mummra moment. 'Croikey!' I thought in my best Steve Irwin accent, 'Take it easy little fella! He's gitting a little bit loively!' But I sensibly kept my mouth shut and hence avoided getting my ass jujitsu'd into 2010. He stayed in Mummra mode for the rest of the journey, so me and Lewis treated him with kid gloves.

Chapter 10
HOMESICKNESS

'Every day's an endless stream/ Of cigarettes and magazines
And every stranger's face I see reminds me that I long to be/
Homeward bound.
I wish I was/ Homeward bound.
Home, where my thought's escaping
Home, where my music's playing
Home, where my love lies waiting
Silently for me.'
Paul Simon, 'Homeward Bound'

Every pre-gapper worries about being homesick. Here is a fairly comprehensive list of the things most people worry about being homesick for: pets, family members, favourite TV soaps, Cheerios, pork pies, flock wallpaper in pubs and curry houses, Carole Vordeman, Cheesy Wotsits, bank holidays in B&Q. There, I don't think I missed anything out, but if so just add it in where you see fit.

If you're taking a post-university gap year, chances are you've already had to come to terms with homesickness, to some degree or another. A recent study on homesickness among British university students showed that 35% of new students experience some homesickness, with between 5% and 15% of these describing the experience as 'frightening'.

But whether or not it's your first experience of being away from home, you're bound to be apprehensive about how much you're going to miss everything that's familiar and dear to your heart (and it's amazing how many things which weren't particularly dear to your heart suddenly become so when you think about leaving them behind).

The good news is most gappers are surprised to find they hardly miss home at all. The excitement of being somewhere completely new, and constantly on the move, leaves little time for leafing through dog-eared, tear-spattered photos or listening to the same old song on your iPod shuffle on one continuous loop. Besides, with even the most remote of places seeming to boast at least one Internet outlet, there's no reason to feel cut off from everything familiar. Dhruti Shah's experience is pretty common.

> I didn't really suffer any homesickness because it was easy to go into an Internet cafe and just access the world from a computer. Also, I was so busy trying to pack in as much as I could during the trip, I didn't have time to feel homesick. I did miss certain British items, including dairy milk – believe me, UHT certainly doesn't compare – and Heinz ketchup.

But no matter how busy and well adjusted you are, there will come a moment when you're feeling particularly low and vulnerable – perhaps when you find yourself sharing a hostel dorm with the World's Loudest Snorer and a couple in training for the sexual Olympics – and your thoughts will turn to home. Gapyear.com's Tom Griffiths warns:

It's quite likely that you will be homesick at some point while you are away. It's only natural and something that, oddly enough, many people are embarrassed about. Maybe it's seen as a sign of failure to admit that you're missing home. In going travelling you've made a bold statement of independence and homesickness may seem like you're backtracking in some way. This is not the case, though. We've all got roots, and the level of attachment to them varies between individuals. Just because you still feel closely allied to where you're from doesn't mean that your quest for independence has failed.

According to a University of Reading Counselling Service leaflet, homesickness was first spotted among Swiss mercenaries in the 1600s and was labelled the 'nostalgic disease'. It was thought to be triggered by singing round the campfire at night – a subversive activity which was immediately banned. The leaflet continues:

> Today we recognise homesickness as a 'syndrome', that is, a phenomenon that has its roots in factors which combine in different ways and with different 'weightings' depending on an individual's background. Homesickness could readily be said to be a form of post-traumatic stress disorder.

Now that should immediately put any worried gapper's mind at rest. Even if you do succumb to homesickness, it's not a form of wussiness, but a full-blown, medically recognised syndrome. Result! The leaflet goes on to list the typical symptoms of homesickness:

- Episodic or constant crying
- Throwing up
- Difficulty sleeping
- Difficulty eating
- Disrupted menstrual cycle
- Absentmindedness
- Unpredictable waves of emotion
- Trembling
- Far too hot or far too cold
- Unable to concentrate or memorise
- Nausea
- Dizziness
- Severe headaches

TRAVELLER'S TOP TIP

Keep thinking of the bigger picture, advises Tom Griffiths.

While you're away you will make many new friends and maybe visit a whole variety of places in a short period of time. You'll also adapt very quickly to a new way of life (whether nomadic or static) and new cultures to boot. By the time you come back, you'll probably be homesick for 'travel' and 'being away' – you'll miss meeting people and visiting places on a regular basis. Being static and part of a community with responsibilities and commitments can be very odd when you return. It is only then that you will wonder what you were worried about in the first place.

Homesickness

Anything can trigger off a bout of homesickness. For many it's feeling under the weather, or a particularly intense phone call back home. Or, as Helen Woodward recalls, it could be something as simple as a song (often not even one you particularly like!):

> The next bout of tears was in a bar in Singapore. We were the only white Westerners in a bar full of Malay and Chinese people. A band was playing well-known covers. The song that got to us both at the very same time was the Bangles hit 'Eternal Flame'. Don't know why but we both started sobbing quietly into our drinks. We were exhausted, though – it had been a very long day... and a very tiring flight. Our defences were low! (Every time I hear that song now, it takes me right back to that night in the bar, feeling homesick).

How unlucky can you be – homesick AND forced to count 'Eternal Flame' in your memorable tracks list for the rest of your life! Life can be so unfair. Tom Griffiths, a gap year veteran himself, acknowledges that when it comes to homesickness, there's no rhyme or reason to what causes it. One minute you're authoritatively negotiating the traffic in Mexico City or breezily zipping off to your teaching job on a tuk-tuk and the next you're sobbing into your sarong at the sight of a hairdo that reminds you of your gran.

> The likelihood is you will miss something, but what that is could be anything – conversations with mates, the colour of the road signs, carpet under your feet, people speaking your language, TV adverts, recognisable money – anything. In fact, trying to judge

what you will miss is difficult, as you'll never know until it happens.

We all like comfort, we all like things we know well and understand. Home is safe – home is easy. Move away from it for a bit and you soon realise where you've come from. To be honest, you miss home most when things go wrong or when you're ill. Birthdays and Christmas can be low points too. If you are miles away from home, you sometimes feel miles away from home. We are all the same.

Constant travelling can sometimes make you feel like you exist in a protected bubble, just you floating along in front of an ever-changing backdrop. But occasionally news from home can pierce the bubble and force you to reconnect, even momentarily, with the *'you'* you were before. Former gapper Helen Woodward says:

A homesick black spot for me was receiving a letter from an old boyfriend who told me he was getting engaged. That really did upset me and make me wonder what I was doing and what might have been had I stayed at home. I remember wandering around Adelaide like a lost soul, in an absolute daze with no one to talk to about the way I felt. That hurt a lot and was one of my really low points.

Quite often, it's the people who go for the 'staying in one place' gap year option who experience the most intense homesickness – because once you get past the fact that, 'Hey, the flat is in Sydney! And I can have my photo taken on Bondi Beach! And it's summer at Christmas-time!' then what you're most likely left with is living in a flat that probably isn't as comfortable as home, doing a job (if you're lucky) that's probably more boring than the one you'd do at home, and mixing with people who wouldn't necessarily be your friends if you were at home. A sure recipe for homesickness, as Emily Reid, twenty, discovered:

Looking back, I think I should probably have taken a gap year after university rather than before. Then I'd already have lived away from home and it wouldn't have been such a shock. As it was, I woke up one morning in my lovely comfy bed in Hove, with my mum making me a cup of tea, and two days later I was landing in Australia, friendless, tear-stained and wondering what the hell I'd done.

I really spent the next six weeks – right up until I found a job and a few friends – alternating between being on the brink of tears, or actually in tears. I was staying with friends of my parents, but I didn't know them very well and I felt as if I should stay out of the house as much as possible. I spent my days sitting in coffee bars watching other people having fun and imagining what all my friends back home would be doing. At night, I'd make long phone calls to my parents. Sometimes I'd be completely silent for ten minutes or more – too miserable to speak. My dad did offer to pay to get my ticket changed so I could come home, but I couldn't bear the shame of showing my face back at our local pub just weeks after I'd had my grand farewell party there. I knew I had to stick it out, no matter how homesick I was.

Contrary to popular myth, homesickness isn't a sign of weakness or a result of being breastfed until the age of ten; it's one of the most fundamental of human emotions. Poets write about it, blues artists sing about it. It affects soldiers, hardened prisoners, even professional footballers on away games. So the first thing to remember is not to beat yourself up about it. Go ahead and wallow for a while – listen to those 'tug at the heartstrings' songs, take out the necklace made from your nephew's baby teeth (but preferably not in public unless you want to be up on a voodoo charge). Often a good bout of self-pity is all it takes to get you back on track again. But there again, not everyone is the same, as Tom Griffiths points out:

> If all gap travellers get homesick at some point, but don't come storming home early, then there must be a few ways of getting over it. These are as diverse as the people who go travelling and if it happens you'll soon discover what suits you.
>
> There is a basic division regarding a cure for homesickness. Some people will find that phoning home, sending a few extra emails and postcards (and asking for some in return) will help, but for others it will add to the problem; they'll prefer to ride it out and get in touch only when they're feeling better about things. Mementos and photos either carried round or sent out to you may also help.

TRAVELLER'S TOP TIP

Ryan Price and Helen Woodward say: 'Stay Connected!'

RYAN: Cy and I don't really miss the UK although we both miss family and friends a lot. It can be hard not having a support network and we've each had bouts of feeling very far from home and missing people. Calling home regularly really helps combat those feelings, and phone cards here in Australia are really cheap. We have bought Oz pay-as-you-go SIM cards, so can also text regularly which is also a good way to keep in contact – and reasonably cheap.

HELEN: Regular phone calls home were the only lifeline. Email didn't really exist back then and we didn't have mobiles so things were very different from the way they are now, where you can really stay in constant touch with everybody back home. If you were on the road in the 1980s, the only way you could get communications from home was via Poste Restante. I do remember huge bouts of disappointment arriving at various post offices around Australia and later in New Zealand to find that no one had written to me. I also remember how happy a quick letter from England could make me feel.

It doesn't matter how long or how meticulously you prepare for a gap year. Occasionally, just occasionally, it's a case of wrong place, wrong time, and when that happens there's little else to do but cut your losses. Gapper Jenny Dodson spent months saving for a trip-of-a-lifetime to Fiji, but when she got there a combination of terrible weather and creeping homesickness caused her to rethink her plans as her gapyear.com diary reveals:

> This was one of my worst days since arriving in Fiji. It was raining when I woke up and was raining when I went to bed. Normally it would stop for an hour or so, but today it was constant. I felt extremely down and homesick. You could see how beautiful this place was and it would be paradise if the sun came out. The whole day was spent being cold and doing nothing. I was seriously considering coming home.
>
> The beaches were beautiful. But now everything started to look all the same. What I have seen and done in Fiji has been amazing and different, but I was starting to think that now I have seen all I want and I'm ready to go home. When I booked to stay here for five weeks I didn't think I would run out of things to do. I thought that when travelling around Fiji I would see loads of different things, but everything here is pretty much the same. So I had decided to give our airline a ring and see if I could get a flight back a week early.

Or sometimes the pull of home can be just too great, as Helen Woodward's travelling companion discovered: 'Lana left Australia after just three months – she missed her boyfriend. I on the other hand was having the time of my life and ended up travelling for eleven months in all. I did get homesick but never so much that I considered throwing in the towel.'

It takes guts to cut short a foreign jaunt. Let's be completely honest for a second – one of the great perks of a gap year abroad is how jealous it makes all your friends. Why else do you spend hours tracking down Internet cafes in the desert, the jungle or the Australian bush just so you can send home photos of 'Me on a beach that looks like the one in the film *The Beach*', 'Me with loads of fit birds/blokes', 'Me scuba diving/bungee jumping'. You want everyone else to know just how great a time you're having, and knowing that they're all wishing it was them somehow makes your own enjoyment even greater. But it works both ways – for someone suffering from homesickness on the other side of the world from all their friends and family, being told how lucky they are can be like a knife in the gut. Half of you wants to live up to the carefree globetrotter image, while the other half just wants to start blubbing down the phone and begging to come home. Samantha Joly is another one who felt the pressure of other people's expectations when she started her new life Down Under. She explains in her gapyear.com diary:

> Now I know you're all expecting me to be having a fantastic time and making loads of friends, etc., but the fact is, being all by myself in a big city isn't quite as easy as I thought it would be! I don't know what possessed me when I decided that I would get along just fine in an empty house as soon as I arrived! I was at a job interview yesterday (went well, have a second interview today, wish me luck!) and met this Irish guy – he was amazed at how brave I was to stay in a house all by myself! He's staying at the YHA in Sydney and he said that even though he's been out on youth hostel organised evenings and is staying in a room with about twelve people, he still feels really homesick, so imagine what I feel like when I get home to an empty house and no one to talk to!

Mostly though, homesickness is pretty much a case of 'now you feel it, now you don't'. One day all you can think about is how you used to love lying in bed with your boyfriend on a Sunday morning reading the papers, and the next you can't remember whether he had blue eyes or green. Usually all it takes is a quick wallow, maybe a sniffly phone call home, and then onwards and upwards, as Rebecca Rowley's gapyear.com diary bears out:

> Well, I've arrived, flight was awful, like reaaaallly bad. Boredom has taken on a new level, although the people on the plane were so easy to talk to (I had a conversation with a Swiss girl in a completely mangled mess of French, German and English). I'm now in the hostel, and it's really scary. Had a bit of whinge after I rang the parents. It's a damn big city and as Donkey says in *Shrek*: 'I'm all aloooooone.' Time for some friend-making methinks.

Chapter 11
LOVE, FRIENDS, RELATIONSHIPS

'I have found out that there ain't no surer way to find out whether you like people or hate them than to travel with them.'
Mark Twain

Gap years can make or break a relationship. Harsh but true. And that goes for friends as well as romantic attachments. The relationships you leave behind can disintegrate, the ones you take with you can go stale and the ones you form over the duration can turn out to be like something out of *Single White Female* or some other movie where someone who seems normal at first turns out to be a knife-wielding psychopath.

Conversely, ties with home can grow stronger through constant emails, phone calls, and letters; friendships with travelling companions can deepen with each new bonding experience; and you can end up with new life-long buddies all over the world.

Like everything in this life, you don't get anywhere without taking a risk, and in actual fact, the risks in this case are pretty small. Real friends won't desert you just because there's a few thousand miles keeping you apart, true love will endure, and if you meet people you don't like, the joy of transiency is you just ditch them at the next bus station.

THE ONES YOU LEAVE BEHIND

Romantic partners

Most precarious among the gap year relationships are romantic involvements that predate the gap year. I mean, it's not an easy thing to accept, is it? 'Sorry, love, can't do our usual takeaway pizza in front of the telly next Friday night, or the next fifty after that, as I'll be travelling the world, meeting exciting new people and seeing exotic new sights.' What do you think the response will be? 'Oh, I'd better switch to a medium-thin crust then if it's just me'. Don't think so.

'However tactfully you break the news, however strong your relationship, the fact that you've decided to go away is bound to feel like a rejection,' says sex and relationships psychologist Dr Petra Boynton.

The truth is that, even if you were planning your gap year long before you met your beloved, it's still going to be a blow to the ego that you're not prepared to take your rucksack back to the shop, tear your ticket into pieces and declare you'd rather stay with them. This is where many hard decisions have to be made, although sometimes gap years provide a useful excuse for a hard decision you'd actually already made in your head. Here's Liz Ely's gapyear.com diary:

> Talked to my boyfriend about 'what we are going to do', something that I have been putting off for a while and we have decided that splitting up is the only option. If I were going away for a shorter length of time, and if I weren't going to Edinburgh University (he lives in

Leeds, by the way!) immediately after I get back, trying to 'make it work' might be possible – but as it is...

I had already come to this conclusion on my own, so it was such a relief to find out that we both feel the same way. It's also really strange as I am now in a relationship with a time limit. It's really odd, because, well, when do we split? The day I go? It also feels like in some ways I could have lengthened our relationship – as we might have split up in the next three months, but now there is no point – might as well avoid the hassle!

I think going away and not thinking I have a boyfriend back home will help me not to feel as homesick, as what I will be thinking about won't be there. However, leaving all my family and friends and ending a relationship of two years all on the same day will be... hmm, well emotional to say the least! Plus it seems unfair to both of us to expect to stay faithful for that amount of time.

In many ways I guess I'm glad it's turning out like this – no difficult decisions to make, no fall-outs or bust-ups – it will be much easier to stay friends. Still seems like a pain though... lots of stupid tears.

When people ask the question 'What are you going to do about Joe?' (which they ask all the damn time, mostly people I don't know that well, too – nosy!), they are disappointed when I tell them 'We're going to split up'. It isn't the answer they want to hear; they want to believe in young love that transgresses time zones, they don't want to be realistic about it. Someone has to be, though.

To be perfectly honest staying together this year would be the easy part (for me at least) and if it were just this one year I could do it – but I am going to

Edinburgh immediately upon my return and I know in my head I won't want to be tied to a boyfriend in Leeds.

Sometimes it's the gap year itself that becomes the reason for the split, other times the gap year just acts as a catalyst for a break-up that would have happened anyway. But at least you've got something to take your mind off your broken heart. And you might even find that having to start off on the adventure without the safety net of a sweetheart stoking the home fires, makes you a stronger person. Jenny Dodson obviously did, as her gapyear.com diary records.

So now I am at the one-week mark before my diving adventure begins in Thailand. My feelings about the trip have changed since I last wrote about it. I recently split from my long-term boyfriend which has had a serious effect on me. I always had plans in my head that involved him, and still do, so coming to terms with the fact he is no longer in my future has been hard. I have tried to keep my head high and some days are better than others, as I'm sure many people will agree. Though now that my trip is only a week away, the scary thoughts of being alone have crowded my mind.

But tonight, as I was watching TV, I decided that it was time to come out of the coma I've been living in for the last few days and look ahead to whatever may be out there. I'm the kind of person who likes to have some kind of plan for the future and now that it's out of my hands, I guess all I can do is give in to whatever may happen, however much it scares the shit out of me!

TRAVELLER'S TOP TIP

Don't be joined at the hip, says Dhruti Shah:

I was very lucky as I was travelling with a friend from university. We gave each other space and although the two of us are Virgos and are stubborn and enjoy a healthy debate, somehow we didn't fall out at all during the trip. I honestly think this is because we made sure we were not spending all our time together. One time I went and did a three-day massage course in Chiang Mai, while she chilled out with some other travellers.

Friends

When it comes to friends, most will be happy to live your adventure vicariously through you, but occasionally it can be as traumatic to leave friends behind as lovers (as discussed in Chapter 3), particularly when their natural jealousy is disguised as criticism or snideness. Ex-gapper Dani Webber recalls:

The only bad thing about the time I spent in Australia is that it changed my relationship with my best friend. We'd always done everything together and she couldn't accept that I was doing this huge thing on my own, even though she'd had the chance to come as well. Over the course of my time away, I rang her loads of times, but she was always really funny with me. Like if I said it was hot where I was, she'd say, 'Oh, I really hate hot weather', or if I said I'd met a really cute guy, she'd always have met someone loads cuter just down the road. In the end I stopped bothering.

THE ONES YOU TAKE WITH YOU

Romantic partners

What could be more romantic – you and your boy/girlfriend exploring the world together, experiencing dramatic sunsets, culture-packed cities, mountain treks, safaris, side by side twenty-four seven? Or, how about this scenario... what could be less romantic – you and your boy/girlfriend experiencing endless bouts of diarrhoea, claustrophobic dorm rooms, jealousy, resentment, mind-numbing boredom, side by side twenty-four seven?

The fact is that when you decide to go travelling with a Love Interest, you have to expect a fair smattering of both scenarios, and it can put even the strongest of relationships to the test. Dr Petra Boynton advises couples to think long and hard before making the decision to do a joint gap year.

> Sometimes one partner will make the decision to go and end up suggesting the other comes along just to avoid hurting them, which can be pretty dangerous. Being together twenty-four hours a day without the support network of friends and family around can put a serious strain on a relationship.

Josie D (she'd rather not be identified) thought that going travelling for a year with her long-term boyfriend would be a safe bet.

> After all, Phil and I had been together since our first term at uni. We'd shared holidays together, illnesses together. I knew his family, he knew mine. We thought we were pretty solid. And our year travelling was going to be a last bit of recklessness before we settled down together and did the house, marriage, children bit.

What they hadn't counted on was the way travel can sometimes unleash parts of your personality that normally stay under wraps.

> To be honest, Phil and I had always had quite an unbalanced relationship where he took the lead most of the time and I was happy to let him. Being away and meeting up with lots of other people my age who were travelling independently and just having a real laugh made me realise that Phil was actually quite controlling and that it was quite likely I'd have a much better time without him. Telling him I wanted to split up when we were staying with friends in New Zealand was the hardest decision I ever made – but also the best.

That's not to say that all couples who travel together unravel together. In fact, if you crack the travelling together nut, you can crack basically anything and you're pretty much obliged to stay together for life because, hey, who else would have held you steady over a squat toilet after one too many Singha beers? Ian Taylor was aware of the pitfalls of travelling with his girlfriend, but a few months into the trip, is very glad he did (gapyear.com):

> We lived together for about seven or eight months before we came away so we knew we wouldn't kill each other when we came away. That said, at home we were in work all the time whereas here we're together twenty-four seven, so there's always going be times when we do each other's head in.
>
> But travelling is such a laugh. We're on the move constantly and there's always loads to see and do – and

it's great to have someone to share it with and reminisce about it all when we get home.

We'd heard loads of stories about couples breaking up because of travelling, but I would definitely recommend it – having an awesome time.

Even if you haven't been together long, a joint gap year doesn't necessarily have to spell premature curtains for your relationship – just be prepared for a few 'getting to know you, fast' hiccups, as Becky Knott discovered when she went away with new boyfriend Jay (gapyear.com):

This is so scary, I've been backpacking before but I was with my girl friend, this is a much bigger deal travelling with Jay. So much to think about: will we be okay together, how will we cope being together so much, will it be harder to get to know other people because we are travelling as a couple?

… Fast forward a little…

Luckily we are getting on better. It was always a risk coming away with Jay after being together for so little time, but being friends for a while definitely helped, and even though we have had a good few arguments and some times when we've both said we wanted to just end it, I'm so glad we haven't (not sure how Jay feels, hopefully the same though!). Most of the arguments have been my fault, I do admit that, due to me being stroppy and my dislike of him smoking like a chimney out here. I should have said something before! But it's all sorted now and like I said, we are better than ever. It's going to be weird not being with him twenty-four seven when we get back; out of nearly two months we have spent about three days apart – that's a lot of time together! It's scary and really making me wonder how the hell we did it!

And for those who manage to explore both the world and each other and come home still enamored of both, the rewards are countless. Jane Yettram married the boyfriend she spent her gap year with, and counts their shared travelling memories as part of the glue that holds them together.

> We'd been together for seven years before we went so we knew each other very well. And this is going to sound pathetic, but there weren't any bad bits! I guess that's why we're now married with two sons! The best thing was the feeling that we were taking a little bit of home with us in each other so even when the travelling was tough or things went wrong, we had some security. And that when we came back, and even now thirteen years later, we can reminisce and share those memories. Experiences are more intense when shared.

Friends

Travelling with friends rather than lovers is in many ways simpler... with the exception of the other ways, in which it's harder. The three biggest mistakes people make when choosing to spend a gap year with a friend are:

1. Selecting on the basis of convenience rather than common ground, as in: 'I know I don't know Luke very well and it is a bit alarming when he does that thing with his front teeth, but he's free from January to July (NB If someone has a suspicious amount of unassigned time, always ask

yourself why) and he knows how to order a beer in Spanish <u>and</u> Mandarin'.

2. Believing that the things that really annoy you about someone at home will magically disappear when you're overseas and therefore liberated from the stresses of everyday life (just think of all those new stresses).

3. Persuading a reluctant acquaintance to come with you just because you're too scared to go on your own – then being lumbered with them the entire trip.

Harriet Chambers' gap year plans had to undergo considerable readjustment when she and her travel-mate Chloe went their separate ways in Vietnam. She says in her gapyear.com diary:

> Initially the plan was that Chloe and I would leave Ho Chi Minh City the day after my dad flew home, taking the train up to Danang, heading to Hue for Christmas and then going on up to Hanoi to meet up with some of the others before she flew home, when I would then go on with my travels as planned. However, another event changed the plans! Chloe and I fell out. Obviously, living in one room together for the last few months and spending what was essentially twenty-four hours a day together had resulted in some minor disagreements. This time, however, it was a different matter and was essentially irreconcilable. So with my dad due the next day I moved into his hotel! All very dramatic stuff!

Zoe Jeanes thought that travelling with friends she'd known half her life would make her immune from Gap Year Bust-ups – boy, was she wrong:

A low point was when me and Fi, who I'd been travelling with for the entire time, had a massive falling out in New Zealand. We'd just got to Queenstown, the crux of our time in NZ, and had had a lot to drink, which was essentially the only reason we argued. Having gotten on each others nerves here and there, the alcohol which coincided with Queenstown just made us a bit more volatile and as such we did have a big argument. The next morning, however, we just talked everything through and it was all as fine as it was before.

It's important to highlight that if you are going travelling with someone else, you need to pick the right person. Me and Fi have been friends for fourteen years, twelve when we went travelling together, and had had every argument/problem/discussion under the sun and knew each other upside down and inside out. I mean, obviously it's fine to go with people you don't know THAT well but this is an important experience, the best of your life, so you've got to make sure that you're going to share it with someone who has similar interests, lifestyle and outlook as you do so that you don't hold each other back.

When it works out well, travelling with a friend or group of friends from home can be the kind of rite of passage Hollywood turns into feelgood movies starring Lindsay Lohan or Hilary Duff. Whatever happens when you get home, whether you all go off to different universities or embark on different careers, you'll always have Rio and Queensland… and that town you can never remember the name of where James tried to chat up the Girl-Who-Turned-Out-Not-To-Be. And when it works out *really* well, you'll be able to take time off alone, regroup, even decide to go on solo, without worrying about upsetting the dynamics or even just upsetting *people*. Haven't got a clue what I'm talking about? Oh, that makes two of us then... Luckily Joe Bloomfield does, because he found himself facing the prospect of cutting his trip short or going on solo after his two travel-mates from home had to bail out early. He says in his gapyear.com diary:

When Lewis, Andy and I planned our trip all those months ago, I never thought I'd end up travelling alone by the end of it. If I'm honest, at the start of our travels the idea of going it alone would probably have filled me with dread. Now I find myself in exactly that position. Nobody to watch my back, nobody to share a room with, nobody to talk to, nobody to travel with.

If at the start I'd known that I would be faced with this situation, I probably would have planned to cut my trip short and go home at the same time as the other guys. I've never been a particularly independent decision maker, you see, so the idea of finding my way through a few thousand miles of foreign territory, with foreign languages that I know barely three sentences of, and alphabets that I can't read, would have scared me off. In fact, it would probably have led me to do a Dr-Zoidberg-style scuttle and yelp to the relative safety of my sofa where I would have switched on *Countdown* (God rest his soul), hidden under some blankets and waited until all this nonsense about going travelling had blown over. However, things can change, including my attitude.

'I give you a week,' Andy said to me after he'd

broken the news that he had to go home. I chuckled to myself. 'What, before I follow you home?' I said, thinking he doubted I'd be able to hack travelling on my own for any length of time. The thought had never even crossed my mind about going home. I was actually quite looking forward to the challenge of going it alone, as sad as it is that Andy has had to cut it short.

'No,' said Andy, beaming smugly, 'I give you a week before you're dead' – and then laughed at his joke for about the next ten minutes. I'm really going to miss him.

THE ONES YOU MAKE ALONG THE WAY
Friends
It is a truth universally acknowledged that anyone travelling for a substantial amount of time will make friends/relationships along the way. Some of these will be soul mates. Others will be no-mates, who latch on to you and refuse to be shaken off. Some would have been mates back at home, others are like exotic birds – fabulous in a specific environment, but wouldn't travel well. Some you'll hook up with for weeks that seem like days, others for hours that drag on like years. And the great thing is, that when you're in constant motion, none of it seems to matter, as Zoe Jeanes explains:

> The one main thing I got out of my travelling experience was the chance to meet some truly brilliant people in the most amazing of places. The thing people have got to understand is that not all of these people are going to become permanent fixtures in your life, and that's fine – they were just fantastic to have around when that particular song was playing, at that particular place, when that particular joke was made.

The moment may not extend much beyond the present and the past but it sits tight in your memory as a golden moment that shines.

TOP TEN LIST OF THINGS THAT SHOULD PUT YOU OFF A POTENTIAL TRAVEL BUDDY

1. No sense of direction
2. Prone to reciting whole episodes of Little Britain
3. Carries a photo of her cat in her wallet
4. Doesn't like heights/planes/confined spaces
5. Gets travel sick
6. Describes herself as 'bubbly' (i.e. will pick up inappropriate hangers-on and bring them back to your room)
7. Unable to carry out basic mental money conversion ('What, you mean I just gave the taxi driver £200? Doh! I thought it was £20!')
8. Snores
9. Doesn't really like 'foreign food'
10. Uses sneaky words like 'em' and 'xi' in Travel Scrabble (sorry, guys, I know they're in the dictionary, but it's still CHEATING)

Of course, you don't want to overdo it with the new mates malarky. No man is an island, true enough. But then no island wants to get overcrowded – just ask Jack and the gang from the cult TV series *Lost*. When travelling it pays to choose your friends wisely and not to let yourself get drawn into a group so unwieldy that you end up being unable to make a spontaneous decision without someone saying 'Let's have a vote on it'.

Love, Friends, Relationships

The truly marvellous thing about travelling is that, when it comes to friendships, it gives you two great powers – to make friends very quickly, and to lose them just as fast. Emily Barr used both those gifts during her travelling years:

Travelling companions are fabulous, and several of my very best friends now are people I've met on the road. I recently had to turn down the chance of being a bridesmaid for Jeff, who I met in Thailand and travelled with for six weeks or so, seven years ago – at his wedding to Cherie who he met in Mozambique (I would have been there like a shot if I hadn't been pregnant, but the wedding was in Florida and I wasn't allowed to fly). In my experience, the further you are from anything familiar, the firmer the friendships with other travellers become. The great joy of it, of course, being that if you don't like someone, you just leave them behind, or go in a different direction.

Once, in Laos, I met a German man who attached himself to me, smoked incessantly, tried to haggle inappropriately in restaurants, and generally annoyed me. I hinted, but he didn't get it. One night he announced that he thought he'd travel with me for a few weeks. So I got up early the next morning and took the six o'clock bus out of town. I still feel a bit guilty – now, I would hope I'd tell him face to face that I didn't want to hang out with him any more – but I must confess I giggled to myself as the bus pulled out of town. Inevitably, I spotted him months later in a bar in Goa, and hid behind a tree until he'd left.

Romantic partners

Romances en route are even more fraught with potential for being either bliss or blunder. Somehow, feelings seem more intense when you're out of your comfort zone, and without work or study or family to provide a distraction, it's all too easy to immerse yourself in a new romance to the obliteration of everything else – which can sometimes be a case of too much too soon. Former gapper Gemma Lester says:

> I remember meeting this one guy at a bar in Cape Town. I was going to be there for a couple of weeks as I was waiting for my sister to join me. Everything about our meeting was perfect – the setting, the timing. We just kind of fell into each other's arms – and stayed there for two weeks, not even coming up for air. But when my sister finally arrived, it was like a spell had been broken. As soon as he was out of earshot she said to me, 'Doesn't he remind you of that creepy guy that used to work behind the counter at Blockbuster?' And immediately I saw she was right. And nothing was quite the same after that.

SEXUAL HEALTH

Along with the sarongs and the carved elephants, there are two souvenirs you probably won't want to bring back from your travels: a sexually transmitted disease or a baby. Dr Petra Boynton, an expert in sexual health, has this advice for female gappers:

• **Sort out contraception well in advance. Go for a coil or** a sufficient supply of the Pill to last throughout your time away.

- Be aware that travelling through time zones can play havoc with the timing of taking the Pill.
- Whatever method of contraception you choose, also take plenty of condoms. Even if you don't end up using them, there will always be someone else who'll be grateful for them.
- If you're prone to cystitis or thrush, take packs of cystitis drinks or Canesten cream with you as these can be hard to get hold of in some areas.
- Research the countries you're going to beforehand. Ask 'Where would I go to for help if I got a sexually transmitted disease or if a condom split?' Make sure you're prepared.

Dr Petra Boynton warns that feelings about a new partner can feel heightened in unfamiliar surroundings. 'Be aware that if you're in a place where you don't know anyone, you'll form very intense relationships, which may leave you quite vulnerable.'

Getting attached to a local carries its own particular set of issues. Dr Petra says:

On one hand it's great because it's a chance to immerse yourself in the local culture, but on the other hand you have to be very careful to avoid misunderstandings. Where there are two different cultures, there are likely to be two different interpretations. Even people who speak the same language don't necessarily attach the same meanings to situations. You might be thinking this is a great holiday affair, while the other person is imagining you're going to be together forever.

But, as with friendships, where a roving romance works, it *really* works. Here's Emily Barr's inspiring tale (warning, grab a hankie for this one):

As for relationships, I am something of an expert on this subject as I'm now married to someone I met in a bar in Chengdu, in China, and we're expecting our third child.

When I'd left Britain, nine months earlier, I was still upset over a broken relationship and one of the reasons I'd gone away was to clear my head. By the time I reached China, a relationship was the very last thing on my mind, and I was loving travelling on my own. It's a cliché, but it was then, when I was least expecting to meet anyone, that he turned up. James is Welsh, and it turned out that we had actually lived two miles from each other in south Wales for two years as teenagers – but as he's a few years younger than me, I, at sixteen, would not have given him, at fourteen, a second glance!

We travelled together for another few months (if I hadn't met James I would never have gone to Pakistan), and I discovered that it really is true that if you can travel with someone, you can live with them. Travelling, we were together twenty-four hours a day, and within a month we were in Pakistan and pretending to be married so we could share hotel rooms.

We came back together, rented a house in London, and really did get married a couple of years later.

Chapter 12
COPING WITH THE UNEXPECTED

'I know I should have been prepared, but...'
Gappers' refrain

Gap years are such amorphous, ever-evolving, undefinable, wilful entities, it's almost impossible to apply any rules or expectations to them, except this one: always expect the unexpected.

In your normal civvy life, you can more or less predict how a typical morning might go. You get up! You eat cereal! You go to work/school/uni! You... (Sorry, just nodded off for a moment there; hold on while I wipe that string of drool off the keyboard...) On Planet Gap Year, everything is different.

There, a typical morning might go like this: You get up! (Course you do, there's a giant multi-legged thingy in bed with you – and he doesn't look like he's after a long lie-in with the papers.) You eat... well, what exactly is that funny looking yellow stuff you've just been handed, wrapped in a giant leaf? You go to work... or rather, you try to but one of the baby orang-utans you're supposed to be caring for has run off and hidden underneath one of the buildings and you have to stand there for ages trying to coax him out.

Anyone spot the subtle differences in the two above scenarios? Whether you're travelling or volunteering, or doing a bit of both, no two gap year days will be the same, which will mostly be a Great Thing. In fact for many, unpredictability is precisely what they've been looking forward to during all the tedious planning and saving stages. But just occasionally, the unexpected will be something that, like a new James Blunt single, you could really have done without.

Of course you'll already know all about the more unwelcome possibilites, as your parents and more envious acquaintances will have taken great pleasure in talking you through them – at length. You'll have heard about the fish that flies up your willy while you're peeing in the Amazon, you'll have heard about the elephantiasis-carrying mosquitos and the spiders that lay eggs under your scalp. You'll have been warned about robbers who chloroform you as you sleep on the beach and steal your stuff, rapists who prey on blonde girls, and pickpocket gangs who hurl buckets of sick over you and nick your wallet while their accomplices help brush it off. You'll have heard about hurricanes in Mexico, sandstorms in Africa and floods in India. You'll have heard about plague, pestilence, piracy and pillaging... *pillaging*?

The good news is that 99.99% of it won't ever come true. The bad news is that 0.01% of it just might. You're unlikely to come down with Japanese encephalitis, but you're almost certain to get a bout of that most exotic of tropical diseases: The Trots. Similarly, you're very unlikely to be shot, hacked to pieces by a machete or kidnapped by extremist gangs, but you just might be mugged or have your passport stolen. Landslides, volcano eruptions and earthquakes aren't everyday gap year occurrences, but monsoons and electric storms can be.

Coping With The Unexpected

The truth is that these unforeseen incidents, unpleasant though they might be at the time, often become the focal points of your trip – stories to recount at the pub for years to come, moments that forever bond you with your travelling companions. To use an American phrase, 'What doesn't kill you makes you stronger' (or, as my friend Steve says, 'What doesn't kill you makes you a plonker'). If you expect the unexpected, you won't panic when it comes along, and there's a better chance of making it into a Top Traveller's Tale to bore your friends rigid with when you get home.

Former soldier and gapper Charlie McGrath set up Operation Gap Safety to teach potential gappers to think and act safe while they travel, so that they can avoid some of the problems he encountered on his first gap year.

> I went to South America in 1979 when I was eighteen. I landed in Brazil. I can remember rolling up to a grotty hostel and thinking, 'Jesus Christ, what am I doing?' I was arrested in Argentina for wearing a combat jacket. I'd been walking down the road and a jeep appeared. I was bundled into the back and paraded in to see the commander. He wanted to swap his pistol for my jacket. I got hepatitis in Ecuador living in the jungle with a tribe, and in Bolivia I befriended the wrong person – he turned out to be the local cocaine king. Then a fellow Briton asked me to take a present home for his granny. I climbed out of the hotel window and ran off to the bus station.

After travelling with the army for three years and then taking another gap year to Pakistan, McGrath started running safety courses first for journalists travelling abroad and then for gappers.

We teach things like how to recognise what's happening at the first signs of trouble, how to switch on the radar, how to evaluate a threat and avoid it if possible and if not, how to diffuse confrontation; how to avoid making yourself a target, how to reduce the chances of being mugged, how to look confident and avoid trouble.

We give advice on everything: on dealing with environmental dangers, drugs, terrorism; on kit – what to take, rucksacks, water purifying systems, devices to lock your room from the inside; as well as medical info, particularly dealing with diarrhoea.

SAFETY: THE GAP GENDER DIVIDE
Charlie McGrath says:

We get a lot of anxious parents contacting us. Parents of boys are concerned that they're clueless and gormless. Often they're justified. Boys think that because they're top of their school they can cope with anything, but it won't mean a thing in Bolivia. Parents of girls are concerned about them travelling alone, or in twos. But I'm not. At that stage they're thoughtful. They know they're vulnerable, which is a very valuable thing to know. Parents often ask us to ask their girls to dye their hair from blonde to brown. Occasionally we might suggest it as it can make a big difference.

ILLNESS AND ACCIDENTS

Okay, talking about diarrhoea (and believe me, you will spend a disproportionate amount of your gap year talking about this very subject, thinking about it, dreaming about it…), we might as well get this one over with now. Chances are, you or someone you're travelling with will get ill at some point or other during your gap year. And chances are very high that this illness will involve a lot of mad dashes to the toilet and frantic fags-for-loo-paper trading. (Incidentally, when I was in Goa with my friend Roma, she was enchanted by the local dialect and tried to learn as many words as she could. When she came across a young lad calling out '*bo-ger-ole, bo-ger-ole*', she stopped to ask him what this musical sounding word meant. The poor boy looked at her blankly. Yes, he was standing outside a public toilet, and yes, he was selling squares of bog roll.)

Anyhow, I digress. The truth is that if you're going abroad for any length of time, particularly to the less developed parts of the world, you're going to be becoming a lot more intimately acquainted with Mr Crapper's excellent invention (okay, pub quiz anoraks, so there's a lot of evidence that says he didn't invent it at all, but that's like saying there's no such person as Father Christmas – the world is soooooo much nicer if people just let you believe that a man called Crapper invented the loo, and a fat, bearded dude in red comes down the chimney on Christmas Eve). Here's Rhys Ingram's lyrical and warmly sympathetic description of his companion's run-in with the runs (gapyear.com): 'My last posts were slightly hurried as I'm sure you realised. This is because Jon, my travel mate, had just taken his seventh trip to the Internet cafe's toilet in an hour AND IT WAS STARTING TO COME FROM BOTH ENDS!'

Still, at least Rhys and his mate were in balmy South America when they got the call from the great white telephone. Poor Jane

Yettram didn't have that luxury out in India. 'I remember being in Simla (and it was FREEZING) and spending the whole night squatting on a loo, wearing gloves, hat, jumpers, fleeces, with only my poor bottom protruding. Nice!'

And Neil Jones in Brazil had to contend with negotiating raging torrents both inside and out when he developed a severe case of Montezuma's revenge (gapyear.com):

> I had not been feeling too well for a few days, not eating very well, and that night I was as ill as I've been for a long time. High fever, dizziness, and bowels with a life of their own. And with no torch I managed to fall into the river on one of my many visits to the toilet. Spent the rest of the night shivering and wishing for the comforts of home, which you always do when you're feeling low.

The thing about diarrhoea is it can catch you out no matter how smug you're feeling about not taking any chances. If it's not the drinking water, it's the river you swam in. If you're feeling immune because you never touch meat, you'll find the cook who prepared your salad hadn't washed his hands. Sometimes it's 'different air', sometimes it's 'a change in climate'. Everyone will have a different explanation, but the result is still the same: Toilet Time. Gapper James Whitaker prided himself on not taking any risks – until that last Mexican cocktail...

> I'd been in Mexico City and was catching a domestic flight from there up to Tijuana on the Mexico–California border, and then crossing the border overland to meet my father in San Diego.

(This was cheaper than paying the international departure tax for a flight into the US.) I had a last night out with some friends I had made in Mexico by way of a send-off, and had a fantastic time. For my whole time in Central America, I had been impeccably careful about drinking water, wanting to avoid any illness linked to it (standard bottled-water only precautions). Unfortunately, that last night, as the drinks flowed, I relaxed my rule and had a fantastic Mexican cocktail with ice in it.

I slept through the next day without too much trouble. I woke up in the late afternoon and got my things together, believing my flight to be an evening one (I was actually twelve hours out and the flight was at eight o' clock the next morning but that's a different story), and made my way to the airport, with a head full of cobwebs and good (if hazy) memories. Only once I arrived at the airport, and as if on cue as I realised I had to spend twelve hours there overnight, the effect of the bad ice in my drink the night before came home to roost, with a vengeance.

It was the worst night of my life, with constant trips to the fairly uninspiring toilets of Mexico City airport to wretch, a constant pain in my stomach (this was a thousand times worse than normal nausea) and a throbbing head. Illness, regardless of how bad it actually is, is always magnified one hundredfold when you're away from the creature comforts of home. When I finally arrived in San Diego the next morning, my father took one look at me and took me straight to the doctor's. Avoid unbottled water and ice in the drinks!

But of course Gut Rot is only one of many different ways to get ill abroad. And even if they're not life-threatening, or even remotely dramatic, they can still leave you feeling very sorry for yourself and wishing that, like Dorothy in *The Wizard of Oz*, you could just click your (espadrilled) heels together and find yourself back home. Here's Janie Spencer's gapyear.com diary:

> Yes, it has happened, the situation I was absolutely dreading, and believe me it's really not pleasant when you're sick on the road! For four days and four nights I couldn't leave my hostel, I would spend my days glued to my hostel bed, too ill to move with barely enough strength to pull a tissue from the box and the nights wide awake trying so hard not to have a coughing fit and wake the seven other bodies in my dorm! I'm okay now, though, thank goodness... but when you're ill there really is 'No place like home'.

If there's one thing you can always count on when getting ill abroad, it's that you're bound to do it in the world's most uncomfortable bed, surrounded by people who have decided that, hey, wouldn't it be fun to have a really loud all-night party, right here in the dorm? Here's a very sorry-for-herself Becky Knott.

> So we had all day in Cairns last Saturday and then flew to Brisbane and got there at 7 pm, just enough time to check in to the hostel and then go and have some tea. But by this time I could hardly breathe, my head felt like it was stuffed with cotton wool and I definitely couldn't taste, so I think the food was nice (it was a nice little Western-themed BBQ) but honestly, I couldn't tell.
> Then, seeing as I was sooo ill, I wanted to just curl

up and go to sleep, but things are never that easy, are they? We were staying above an English-themed pub that happened to have a live band playing who might as well have been playing at the end of the bed, so after six hours' trying to sleep I finally nodded off about 4 am – even the cold tablets which are supposed to help you sleep didn't work!

And if lying in a strange bed trying to sleep while some Ozzie prog rock band does covers of Led Zep songs on your head isn't your idea of fun, imagine ending up in a foreign hospital like Lara Hallam... Here's her gapyear.com diary:

Yes, you read the intro right – I ended up in hospital in Kuala Lumpur. After feeling really ill I went down to the local hospital. After checking into the hospital I saw the first doctor, who referred me for blood tests, etc. Then I saw a specialist doctor who confirmed I had a bad water infection that had moved up to my kidneys, resulting in a kidney infection! They asked me to admit myself to stay a few nights under observation.

Unfortunately, even in my ill state the receptionist still tried to con me out of money, saying the only bed in the whole hospital was a VIP deluxe costing around £80 a night. Darren was a star and said if that's the only room, we need a letter saying that, otherwise our insurers would not pay back. After much delay a bed appeared on a ward for me! Once on the ward there were only two other people and three free beds – so they must have been lying!

The nurses were fab, they all spoke quite good English and helped me whenever I needed it. After being on a drip for a few days, I got discharged along with a packet of tablets.

Very rarely, and only if you're really unlucky, an illness will get so bad you'll have to change your travel plans, maybe even return home. And sometimes it can start with the most trivial of incidents, as happened with Hannah Bailey in Fiji (gapyear.com):

I've been quite ill over the past few weeks, got a nice selection of disgusting boils going from the top of my leg just past my knee. It all started as one lone mozzie bite; this mozzie bite turned into the boil from hell. Some of the people I stayed with placed a leaf with coconut oil on it. This worked quite well at drawing the pus out, but unfortunately the boil then spread. The reasons people came up with for this ranged from not washing properly to too many people looking at it and giving it bad feeling. Everyone cast an opinion on it and it really didn't help. I then went to a private doctor (don't do it); they charged me $50 to tell me my leg was infected, which was quite obvious considering it was swollen and red. I then got given some really poo antibiotics.

After enduring the ugliness for two weeks, I decided it was time to go to the hospital. This was a brilliant experience in itself. I was expected to share my problems with four other patients who were also waiting in the room where I was being seen to. The doctor, who was very sweet, gave me a really strong course of antibiotics that worked up to a certain extent but I then got blisters on my calf and decided to go back and get some injections. This all worked out cheaper because I met a Fijian girl in the waiting room and they just put it onto her health card.

I was prescribed three days' worth of jabs. The first day was the worst. I passed out from the pain in front of everyone in the waiting room. Luckily I had my new friend with me, and she looked after me. The second was better, although I do think they got my bum out more than they really needed to. I had surely the whitest bum they had ever seen. The third day, the penicillin all came running back out of the jab wound. I also have a severe cough by Fiji standards, although if I'd been at home they would just have given me some cough mixture. Everyone in the hospital waiting room appeared to be there because they had a cough and were coming for their antibiotics. It's so strange, they do think you're dying if you have a cough. So, recently, I have just been sleeping, trying to get rid of these disgusting marks. I will be leaving asap to get to Oz so I can get some reliable treatment.

... *Fast forward several days*... After coming back from yet another visit to one of the islands, I decided it was time to head home. The boils had grown out of control. The whole of my left leg was covered, and to go with these ugly pus mountains I had got a really bad chest infection. My mum asked me to come home – she and dad were really worried that I might get blood poisoning.

It was a pure mission getting home. I went to Auckland from Fiji, then to Singapore where I stayed on standby for fifteen hours before the thirteen-hour flight back to Heathrow, with no in-flight entertainment. Under the pressure of the flight my legs swelled and bled. Unfortunately, in this country it appears everyone only thinks of themselves. I had to struggle through the airport with all my luggage and only one leg to literally stand on.

I'm so gutted to be home, but luckily due to the medical care here my legs are now getting better. A & E found my legs very interesting. They did worry me, though, when they said they wanted to send me to the Hospital for Tropical Diseases.

But if illnesses are bad, accidents are even worse. One minute there you are happily trying to master the word for 'hello' in Vietnamese, and the next you're attempting to explain to some policeman that it wasn't your fault the moped developed a will of its own and to the nurse that you've already had a tetanus jab, thank you very much, and could she please stop waving that very long, sharp needle so near your bottom. Dhruti Shah still carries the scars to remind her of one of her less inspired travelling ideas:

We hired a motorbike when we were in Cambodia, and on New Year's Day 2004 we were involved in an accident. I was stupid and had been riding pillion wearing shorts and my leg was burnt by the bike's exhaust pipe. I just went into autopilot and found a chemist and washed my leg straight away. Then we used the first aid kit we had brought with us from home and bandaged up the burns. I had to attend clinics for the remainder of our trip. Common sense prevails. When you are abroad not everybody is going to speak English and be able to help you, so you have to just take stock of the situation – like we did – and do the best you can in the circumstances. There is no point panicking – and don't put yourself in stupid situations. I've got scars on my leg as a constant reminder.

Being involved in any kind of accident is always a jolt to the system, but when you're in an unfamiliar country, surrounded by strangers, it can border on the surreal as Julian Draper discovered when he came a cropper snowboarding in Queenstown.

After I'd been taken off the slopes on a stretcher following a snowboarding mishap, the doctors had to establish whether or not I was concussed. (For the record: I wasn't. I was fine.) In order to do so they asked me a series of rather stupid questions.

'What day is it?'

'I don't know, I'm travelling, I'm not really keeping track.'

'Oh, okay. What month is it?'

'Hmmm – I think it might be July now?'

'No, it's still June. Who is the Prime Minister of New Zealand?'

'I have no idea. Are you serious?'

'Yes. Is it a man or a woman?'

'If I don't know who it is – how on earth can I know that?'

'Right, you seem to have concussion. You'd better lie here for several hours.'

'Can I have my ski pass money back?'

'No.'

CRIME

There is a certain mythical mathematical equation that goes something like this: young person plus backpack equals moving target. Now, this is not technically correct. There are loads and loads of people who travel all round the world, leaving their stuff on beaches while they swim, asking complete strangers to keep an eye on their bags, and generally taking all sorts of stupid risks, and nothing ever happens to them. But, let's face it. You're in a foreign country, you don't know the ropes, you're sure to be carrying a stash of cash somewhere about your person. If it's going to be anyone, it might well be you.

Cab crime

In the UK, usually the worst crime you can expect when you get into a taxi is to have to listen to a long, convoluted racist joke or be told to cheer up because it might never happen. Abroad it can occasionally be a different matter. That's not to say that all foreign taxi drivers are out to get you, just that it pays to be extra vigilant. Here's Emily Barr:

> The most unexpected thing that happened to me was in Pakistan, when a taxi driver taking James and me from Lahore to the Indian border stopped the car by the side of a quiet country road. There was a group of men there who strode up to my open window brandishing their guns. James had the presence of mind to realise that our only chance of getting away was the cab driver, and he leaned forward and punched him and swore at him until, thankfully, the driver drove off.
>
> I was shaken for ages after that (trying not to let myself imagine what people can do if they've got a gun pointed at you), but it was just another learning

experience. If they'd taken our bags, we could have sorted it out on insurance, and all our money and documents were in money belts. When we reached the border we went to tell an official what had happened, and the cabbie was so scared that he drove off without waiting for his fare.

TRAVELLER'S TOP TIP
Karen Golightly recommends making copies of everything:

Easier said than done but don't panic if something goes wrong – it only makes it worse. Keep focused on the next steps to achieving a solution, whether that be getting medical treatment, police help, etc. Make sure that someone responsible at home (and with access to a fax or PC) has copies of all your important information – flight details, passports, itinerary – and keeps them updated when anything changes.

Oliver Ralph's Chinese taxi driver's crime wasn't so much directed at them, as at the authorities, but it nearly cost him dear anyway...

Chengdu, China, October 1997. Five weary travellers stagger off the train from Xi'an after a twenty-four-hour marathon journey. Disorientated, we selected the first taxi driver who sounded like he had a moderate grasp of English and piled into his cab, rucksacks stuffed into the back. The journey started quietly enough, but the speed soon picked up and before long we were careering down narrow streets, pedestrians and bicycles flying out of our way as we narrowly avoided a major incident. A glance out of the back windscreen revealed that we were being pursued by the police. Our driver, it turned out, did not have a licence and did not actually speak English. A traffic jam came to our rescue. At an enforced stop we grabbed our bags and piled out of the car. We decided to walk the rest of the way.

Petty crime

Pickpockets and muggers can strike anywhere: Berwick, Aylesbury, Buxton (don't look so shocked). The difference is that if you're travelling, you're far more likely to be carrying a lot of valuable stuff – like cash and passports – which is obviously a complete pain to replace, as Vix Carter recounts in her gapyear.com diary:

> I am writing this from an Internet cafe in Kampot whilst Scotty phones the embassy, the police, his parents, STA Travel, STA Insurance, American Express and many more people after he had his money belt stolen in Phnom Penh. And we only realised when we got here. So tomorrow we have to go back to Phnom Penh! Great! And then we have to go back again in two weeks or so to pick up a new passport and visa for a bargain 200 bucks. Woo hoo! Still, I quite like Cambodia despite its insistence on robbing us blind at every turn.

The accepted wisdom if you're being robbed is to hand over the money (excepting the emergency fund you've got stuffed in your shoe or the inside jacket of your guidebook). But just occasionally, there is space for some minor heroics. Here's Jane Yettram's experience.

> We had one attempted theft by a pickpocket in Mexico, but that was foiled. The pickpocket dropped his leather bag on the floor of a bus and as he bent down to get it, he took my boyfriend's wallet. But I saw him take the wallet and managed to grab the pickpocket's bag from the floor. He looked horrified. One look at us probably told him he had a lot more money in his bag than we had in that wallet! (We'd keep a tiny bit of handy cash in the wallet and the rest in our money belts.) So we stared at each other then swapped bag for wallet and he scarpered.

Corruption

Most tricky for many gappers to comprehend is the kind of crime committed by the very authority figures you'd expect to go to for help if you were the victim of a crime. The blunt fact is that in countries where wages are low and corruption widespread, the friendly neighbourhood bobby or helpful, smiling customs officer might not always be what they seem. Friends of mine travelling in Peru a few years back got caught in a classic police sting when they were stupid enough to let a stranger they met at their hotel persuade them to change money on the black market, promising them a better rate than changing money through the official channels.

When they turned up at the prearranged time, they handed over the cash and got in exchange… a plastic bag containing enough cocaine to keep Pete Doherty awake for a very long time. And what do you know, before they had a chance to react, the police were on the scene, threatening them with thirty years' imprisonment, unless they paid them US$1,000. They were driven straight to the airport, which was the only place with functioning cash machines. There, they emptied out their UK savings account, paid off the police and were on the first plane back home the next morning.

In his safety courses, Charlie McGrath tries to pre-warn gappers that the men in uniform aren't always the good guys: 'We talk about the black market, where to change money and the role played by corrupt policemen – alerting them to that fact.'

For Gap Sports' James Burton, it wasn't the police but a border guard who turned out to be not so much upholding the law as withholding it.

> I crossed the border between Zimbabwe and Namibia. I didn't really realise that the border guard had taken my passport and not handed it back. When I got to the next crossing point, I realised I didn't have my passport and had to go back for it. British passports are worth a lot on the black market. The border guard had put it in his pocket.

'WE BROKE DOWN IN THE MIDDLE OF NOWHERE'

This mini case history from Joe Bloomfield on Fraser Island, recounted in his gapyear.com diary, shows that the unexpected doesn't always have to be dangerous...

Off we drove, bouncing about all over the place, until eventually we got to the turn-off. A small, ragged cheer came from the guys in the back. This was soon stifled when a few hundred metres down this track Lewis said,

'What's going on? I've lost power.'

Really not good. We were stopped in the middle of a one-way track in a forest 9 km from the beach, with the clock ticking against us to get the boat off the island, and the car wouldn't start. Apparently it felt as if it had run out of petrol, but the gauge was still showing we had some left. We decided the best course of action was to walk back up to the junction, as there were a couple of other turn-offs there, and flag someone down.

Me, Sunny, Lewis and Rose walked up to the junction and flagged down the first car we saw, ten or fifteen minutes later. Inside were an American tourist family who didn't have any petrol nor, as it turned out, any idea how to work a manual gearbox. The guy stalled it about six times in a row as they were trying to pull away.

The next vehicle we stopped had a ranger guide driving a tour bus full of people, heading down the road we were blocking. This was in no way embarrassing, I promise you. We explained the situation to him and over the microphone he offered his passengers an alternative route. They were meant to be heading to Lake McKenzie and instead they were offered a walk in the woods. Thankfully they obliged, and he told us that he'd drop them off then come round and tow us out of the way.

We arrived back at the car to find everyone sat down on the bank having a nice little picnic. Hmm. We got them to pack up all the stuff in the quickest time possible and soon the ranger turned up with his tow rope, for which we were most grateful. He towed us about 500 metres down the track, to a junction where cars could pass us safely. We thanked him and waved him off, but were now stuck about 8.5 km from Eurong with a boat to catch about 50 km away. (He told us the last one went at 4 pm), so little had improved.

Sunny, Lewis and I decided we'd walk to Central Station (the very centre of Fraser Island), about a mile away from the car, to phone the mechanical support number in the handbook we'd been given. It now being 2 pm, Rose hitched a lift back to Eurong to try to scrounge some fuel and hopefully a lift back to our car.

After paying about ten bucks in the phone, explaining the problem and getting the guy to come out, we turned round and made the long walk back to the vehicle. He'd said he wouldn't be with us until about an hour's time, which would make it half past three. We realised we would never make the 4 pm barge in time, and thought we were going to have to spend another night stranded on Fraser Island.

We trudged back and then spent a bit of time waiting around, kicking a football about and dodging passing cars, who slowed down to do a spot of rubbernecking at us.

Rose then pulled up in a car and out crawled three nasty looking guys with cans of VB and rollies stuck to their bottom lips. They wanted to fix the car for us and were going to give it a going over. We said no, we were getting someone qualified to come out and we wanted to prove that the dial still showed there was some fuel left in it. They demanded fifty bucks off us for wasting their time when they could have been out fixing other people's cars. After a mild protest we paid up, just to get rid of them, seeing as it was only five bucks each.

About five minutes after they left – an exact hour, to the minute, after the mechanic said he was going to be there – up pulled another car. Out stepped Keith.

'What's wrong with 'ere, then?' he cried, striding purposefully over to the business end of the vehicle.

He put the key in the ignition, turned the key and the engine roared into life. Unbelievable. After all that, he just started it first time – how thoroughly embarrassing. Thankfully, the engine spluttered out, so our blushes were spared somewhat. That is, until he gave his diagnosis:

'She's outta fuel, guys. You've run her dry. Now let's get this tow rope on her and get out or we'll miss the boat.'

'Miss the boat? We're miles away, and the last one's at four.'

'Nah, mate, it's at five.'

So off we went, me and a few others sitting in the broken vehicle (with Sunny doing a fine job of steering), a few sitting in the van with Keith as he hared off down the bumpy track in front of us.

We got to Eurong, and Keith told us to put only thirty bucks of diesel in, as it's more expensive there than on the mainland. He then fiddled about under the bonnet, apparently bleeding air out of the engine. The clock was still ticking down and our chances of getting the last boat off the island were diminishing.

We got back in, Sunny driving Keith's car and me

riding shotgun in the van with Keith. On the journey I had a bit of a chat with him and he turned out to be a really friendly guy, with loads of advice on what to do and see in Australia. Our conversation was cut short when his phone rang...

'Ben?' he says (it's his boss). 'Nah, mate, they still had plenty of fuel, it was an electrical problem... Nah, nah, not their fault at all... Them? Yeah, they're okay, mate... Nah, they're not too upset with us... It happens... Okay, mate, cheers... Oh! One other thing, can you ring the barge and get them to wait for us, please?' Then he hangs up.

'Guys, I've just told him that it wasn't your fault, and you didn't run out of petrol, otherwise you'd be paying somewhere in the region of $400 for the call-out and refuelling my car and yours... Also...' (at this point he leant forward on the dashboard and fiddled with it) 'I've just put your mileometer back by 100 km, 'cos you were told that it runs out at 380. You had done 390, now you've only done 290. Also, the barge is going to wait there till 5.30 for us, so we won't miss it.'

Now it may have just been my imagination, or the lack of sleep, or perhaps a few grains of sand in my eyes, but I swear I saw a faint circle of light over his head.

We got to the barge at 5.25 pm. Against all odds we'd made it. We filled up the tank to the brim when we got back to Rainbow beach and handed back the car. Later on that evening we went and found Keith and had a drink with him. As I said at the start of this little story, he's a twenty-four-carat legend.

EVENTS BEYOND YOUR CONTROL

Among the millions affected when the tsunami hit on Boxing Day 2004 were UK gappers, many of them away from home for the first time (see Sarah Cumming's tsunami account, Gap Year Casebook Three in Chapter 16). Of course, nothing can prepare you for an event of this magnitude. But even natural disasters on a much smaller scale can have a massive impact. Here's Sarah Cumming again – this time writing a gapyear.com diary account from Vietnam:

I'm currently stranded in Hoi An at the moment and just waded through knee-deep water to get from guest house to town centre. When I say knee deep, I mean knee deep for most average sized people. Me being only five foot tall, it's more like waist deep. The Vietnamese people who are living here are all very confused. I would love to attach a picture of the flood and their faces but fear that the computer may die. It mentions typhoons in the trusted Lonely Planet guidebook, and in Hue, a town slightly further north, the locals said it always rains and they always have floods. Here people say the same, but from the look on their faces and the organisational farce you would think that they had never even seen rain!

Anyway, I wanted to leave here tonight now that I am feeling better after my four-day bout of gastroenteritis (note to myself – never get sick in Vietnam; they don't even sell mosquito spray so what hope did I have?). But the bus leaving tonight has been cancelled and they don't know about tomorrow yet. They think there may be some sunshine but they're not sure. 'Sun tomollow' has been said for five days now, so

I don't believe there will be 'sun tomollow' and fear that I may be stuck here forever. The nearest airport is an hour away but guess what – no way of getting there either!

I suppose it is quite fun to be wading through floods and watching a mixture of boats and bicycles meander down the road but when I'm recovering from food poisoning and only allowed to eat rice and water and three different 'medicines', it's suddenly not fun anymore.

In Britain we always like to believe we can control the weather – we have brollies to keep out the rain, windbreaks to protect us from the wind. But in countries more accustomed to extreme weather conditions, you learn quickly that it's pointless to try to exert your will against the meteorological might, and you might as well just give in to it, as TV presenter and travel writer Sankha Guha recalls of his experiences:

I was caught in a hurricane in Fort Lauderdale, Florida. At night we toured the Intracoastal Waterway to experience the edge of the storm. The beach was impressive – palm trees bent horizontal, high tide and huge malevolent waves smashing the shore. We went home and had a party, my hosts opened a rare bottle of ancient cognac and we watched the disaster on television. The hurricane stayed a few miles offshore and later pounded West Palm Beach to bits. We were almost disappointed.

But it's not only the weather that's beyond our control. Buses, trains and planes all involve the slight thrill of placing yourself in someone else's hands. Here's Jane Yettram's account of one of her more memorable plane journeys:

> Our one major crisis was the day we took a light plane from Pokhara to Jomsom in Nepal, planning to do a seven-day trek back to Pokhara. The weather was perfect – fine and clear – when we set off. But as soon as we rose above the mountains we were buffeted by an onslaught of wind howling across the Himalayas. The plane bounced and spun and the pilot's knuckles were white as he tried to control it. All we could see were the huge white flanks of the mountains coming closer and closer. Finally, he managed to turn the plane and get us back to Pokhara. But, with the small number of passengers terrified and many screaming, it was a terrifying experience. We were shaky as we got off the plane, but decided the only thing to do was to start the trek, go halfway and then come back (we had a plane to catch to Hong Kong eight days later). So we did.
>
> The mountain air, solitude, tumbling streams – all were soothing. And the meditative rhythm of walking calmed us down. It wasn't until that evening, at the mountain lodge where we spent our first night, that I burst into tears. Delayed shock, I suppose. But being high in the mountains with all the stars, and having started trekking as we'd intended, really helped.

And if you're talking about crises that are really beyond your control, you can't do much better than close encounters of the nasty kind with our animal buddies. James Burton from Gap Sports had several run-ins with furry and not so furry friends (and not so friendly come to think of it...) during his own gap year:

I'll never forget my encounter with one of the world's most dangerous snakes. I went out canoeing in South Africa on my own. As I turned the boat around, there was a brown adder crossing the water, head raised ready to take me. For a split second we just looked at each other. Then I took a deep breath, held the oar up and went past it. As I went past it I could see its head staring me out. It was surreal. I didn't weigh up the consequences until later, after I'd classified the snake. They're big snakes and grow about two metres long – a bite from one of those would kill you in five hours.

Another time, one of the families we were staying with in Zimbabwe had a houseboat on Lake Cariba. A group of us went out in a small motorboat to do some fishing in the late afternoon/early evening. We could see there were lots of crocodiles in the water, but didn't think that much of it even though, as there were six of us, the boat was very low in the water. We got quite carried away catching loads of small tiger fish and before we knew it the sun had set. Then we realised we couldn't start the motor up.

We started drifting past the reeds where we'd been fishing and into the lake itself. Then from nowhere five hippos came up around the boat. These are the deadliest animals to man in Africa and kill more humans than any other creature. They're massive. When they open their mouths and you can see their teeth, you realise just how big they are. We started to panic. They were very close to us. We sat in the boat for an hour or two surrounded by these creatures before a rescue party came out for us and towed us back. With the big lights from the rescue boats, we could see the crocodiles' eyes gleaming in the water.

FROM VOLUNTEERS TO HEROES

It's fair to say that most of the crises you'll have to deal with on your gap year will involve unexpected things that happen to you directly, but occasionally it'll be someone else who's in trouble and you who has to make that split-second decision – to help or to hide. This is the story of gap-year heroes the Mamallapuram Four, as reported by Richard Venning of gap year organisation Africa & Asia Venture:

Adrian Havelock, Aelene Thorne, Fiona Humphrey and Amy Campbell-Golding were travelling in India as part of their gap year placement with Africa & Asia Venture (known to many as AV). The travel was part of the placement, but followed three months' work in the Kangra Valley in Himachal in the foothills of the Western Himalayas. It was early 2000.

They had endured the long train journey from Delhi to Chennai and were relaxing beside the sea at Mamallapuram in Tamil Nadu. They had planned to swim, but the surf was too high and the steeply shelving beach and undertow were worries. So they decided to stay on the beach and sunbathe. They watched a party of office workers from Chennai arrive and ask fishermen on the beach to take them out in one of their fishing boats, pulled up on the sand. Most would not, because of the sea, but eventually one of the boatmen was persuaded and the entire party of men in suits and ladies in saris and high heels boarded and the boat was pushed into the waves. About 40 to 50 metres from shore the boat went straight up a wave and turned bow over stern, tipping all the passengers into the sea.

One of the volunteers saw it happen, yelled 'Come on!' and the three strong swimmers set off to where the passengers, almost none of whom could swim, were struggling in the water or clinging to the upturned boat. They managed to pull in several and brought them to the beach where Amy helped with resuscitating them and other survivors who were also brought in. Some survivors were quickly taught rudimentary CPR in an effort to save more. The volunteers managed to tow in the boat with several survivors clinging to it. However, not all survived, and they also had the terrible task of telling one or two husbands that their wives were dead.

There came a point when they could do no more and so quietly returned to their hotel, moving on the next day. The story was reported in the Chennai newspapers the next day, speculating on the identity of the foreign hero and heroines. The four were all later to receive an award from the Royal Humane Society.

If you were to do a straw poll of the 'beyond your control' situations that would most raise parental blood pressures, the winner would surely be either 'entering a war zone' or 'getting caught up in civil unrest'. But then, who'd be crazy enough to do that? Er, Rhys Ingram apparently (gapyear.com):

We eventually got out of Manaus relatively unscathed and, after realising just in time we were in the wrong airport in São Paulo waiting for our connecting flight, we were at last flying over Bolivia. Immediately I felt an excitement I hadn't felt before – Bolivia seemed a much wilder country than Brazil! It was perhaps this that caused me to laugh off the comment made by a local sitting next to me about hoping our plans went ahead despite the 'protests'.

Due to the exhausting last few days I'd had I really didn't acknowledge this as I should. As we flew over the Andes, which even at night were beautiful, we came over a final mountain and there was La Paz! It was glowing with street lights and truly stunning, especially with the largest local mountain towering over the city and glistening with snow. There was also no sign of any protests going on, which gave me further reason to forget the comment made to me on the plane.

The next morning, however, we woke up to the sound of chanting, whistles and bangers going off! It appeared the warning had been fair enough. We wandered round the city trying to avoid the sounds of the protesters. We stopped for lunch in a small restaurant and as we were eating we heard them coming. The waiter ran to the door and slammed it shut, struggling to hold it closed due to the protesters kicking and knocking everything in their path. With that the waiter's wife decided she'd had enough and ran out of the kitchens into the street to take on the protesters with dishcloth and ladle in hand! Her poor husband was no match for her and it took several people to get her back inside to safety!

We managed to spend the rest of the day in a pretty uneventful manner, and it wasn't until the meeting with our tour leader that we realised how serious this was. We were stuck in La Paz as El Alto, where the protesters were from, was the only route out of the city. Some people had been gassed or were in buses that had been stoned and none of the local bus drivers were willing to take us to Peru where our own tour bus was stuck waiting for us. Any drivers who left the city were reportedly getting taken out of their buses and beaten! We were stuck in La Paz until there was a resolution.

Chapter 13
NIGHTLIFE, THRILLS, FUN

'Enjoy yourself, it's later than you think
Enjoy yourself, while you're still in the pink
The years go by, as quickly as a wink
Enjoy yourself
Enjoy yourself
It's later than you think.'
Prince Buster, 'Enjoy Yourself'

Sometimes, in the midst of the planning and organising, the agonising long journeys, the diarrhoea, the falling out with friends and general boring stuff, it's possible to lose sight of the main thing about a gap year – it's fun.

Now, it may seem slightly odd to use the word 'fun' about a trip that in some cases will involve, say, working with street children in Brazil or land-mine victims in Cambodia, but it's true. Whatever you get up to while you're away, you're going to experience the whole spectrum of emotions from outrage to sympathy to frustration – but in addition to these, and usually far outweighing them, you're going to have fun. Lots of it. And there's no need to feel guilty about it either, even if you are doing a serious placement. Contrary to popular myth, gap year organisations don't require you to relinquish your sense of humour and capacity for enjoyment along with your deposit when you sign on the dotted line. Think about it, who's going to make the better volunteer – someone who bursts into empathetic tears at the sight of suffering, or someone who knows how to raise a smile?

Gap years are about enjoying yourself, and 99.99% of gappers (figures based on a scientific survey of everyone I've spoken to for this book) do just that. In fact, sometimes they do it far too well. Jan Williams says:

> When we lent our son Toby £1,000 towards his gap year trip, we wanted him to have a good time of course, but we also expected him to come back having learned something. But when every email he sent us contained stories of wild nights out and jumping into waterfalls on pieces of elastic, I started to wonder whether he wasn't doing just a bit too much of one and very little of the other!

Jan's son Toby is still, as we go to press, somewhere in Asia having Far Too Much Fun (and if you should run into him, do Jan a favour and tell him to phone home).

For most people, enjoyment contains a certain degree of hedonism, but also a fair smattering of achievement and self-growth. American psychologist Martin Seligman spent decades researching well-being and concluded, in his book *Authentic Happiness* (Nicholas Brealey Publishing), that there are three levels of happiness, which he terms the 'pleasant life', the 'good life' and the 'meaningful life'.

Level one, the 'pleasant life', is all about immediate

gratification – slamming that tequila shot, snogging that guy who looks a little bit like Colin Farrell (if you ignore the bad facial hair), finding that ten quid scrunched up in the bottom of your jeans pocket.

Level two is 'good life', which means finding out your particular talents and making the most of them in your daily life (NB – this is more apt if your special talent is, say, 'writing poetry' or 'motivating others' and less if it involves blowing up condoms over your head).

The third and optimum level of happiness is 'meaningful life', which entails using your particular talents and strengths for the good of other people. Yes, folks, it's official. What makes you happiest of all is using your unique gifts to make other people happy.

Which is all, of course, a roundabout way of saying that you're not only allowed to enjoy your gap year, you have a duty to do so. And those who go for the volunteering option are not only likely to have just as good a time as their 'seventeen pints a night in Surfers Paradise' peers but, potentially, even better. Just something to think about...

So now that's all cleared up and fun is officially back on the menu, it's time to have a look at all the different ways gappers enjoy themselves during their time out. Okay, let's rephrase that, it's time to look at *some* of the ways gappers enjoy themselves (first rule of publishing: it's best not to alienate a large section of your readership or, more specifically, their parents).

NIGHTLIFE... AND THE FAMOUS FULL MOON PARTY IN KOH PHANGAN

Unless you've booked yourself on to a six-month monastic retreat or one of those Thai therapies where you have to go to bed at 9 pm to think pure thoughts and have clay piped up your bottom twice a day, you're going to be experiencing the nightlife of whichever country you find yourself in. And with no 9 am clock-in or 10.30 am lecture to get up for, it's easy to find nightlife morphing into day-life in one endless round of beer and bars. Thank goodness for the holy trinity of: a) common sense, b) willpower, and c) lack of drinking funds.

Still, even if you're not tripping the light fantastic every night, you're going to be trying it out on a few special occasions, and there's none more special in the gapper's diary than the Full Moon Party on the Thai island of Koh Phangan. This monthly event attracts thousands of revellers all sporting their best flip-flops and some have even washed their hair! Sarah Cumming was a somewhat reluctant convert (gapyear.com):

> The Full Moon Party on Koh Phangan was so much better than I expected. After hearing so much negativity about it I was beginning to think I wouldn't bother, but then I always said I would have to try for myself before deciding, and it was brilliant! I think it really got into swing at around 5.30 am but I don't know if this was maybe due to the fact that by then I'd been dancing for nearly twelve hours and drunk nearly twelve buckets of SangSom mix! (No, I didn't really have twelve. I'm not that hard core.)

Helen Bray, on the other hand, needed very little converting. Here's her gapyear.com diary:

> The highlight was of course the Full Moon Party on Ko Phangan – wow! It was sooo much fun! Everyone dances on the beach all night and then all day, drinking buckets of the cheapest whisky in Thailand! I highly

recommend these parties! Especially since there are 'warm up' parties, half moon parties, 'night after the full moon' parties... Every night is a party!

According to www.fullmoon.phangan.info, Koh Phangan is one of the world's 'biggest and best beach bashes'. 'There are few places in this world where you can live out your desert island dreams of palm trees and white sand beaches, and still have a blinding night out at a rocking party every month,' the website points out.

Right at the heart of the Full Moon Party is Haad Rin beach, which apparently boasts twelve major sound systems catering for 8,000 to 12,000 punters in low season, 15,000 to 20,000 in high season and up to 30,000 at New Year. Anyone suffering from a fear of crowds, bright lights, loud noise or the sight of bodies lying groaning on the ground should probably give the place a wide berth. Which is something Rhys Ingram definitely didn't do (gapyear.com):

Eventually the big day arrived and as night fell we started to slip a few beers down and apply luminous paint to our bodies. I know, sounds cheesy and a bit tacky, but trust me, at full moon it works! When we got out we didn't want to peak too soon so chilled out in a few bars in the town before making our way to the beach. The atmosphere was amazing, though – everyone up for a good time but not really knowing what to expect from it all either!

When we did step onto the beach it was rammed, we lost a few people straight away, and slowly a few more disappeared never to be seen again. There must have been two or three times the number of people there compared to previous nights. A few buckets down, though, and it didn't matter anymore. Dancing on tables and stages or wherever there was room ensued and I had the most mad night of my life. It didn't matter how much you danced, you just carried on, the adrenaline rush was intense.

When the sun came up it was like something out of *Saving Private Ryan*. The beach was covered in people walking round in a daze and people laid out on the floor looking half dead, and the bass coming from the drum 'n' bass tent sounded like bombs going off, but there were still some of us who kept on dancing and drinking. At nine o'clock the few people I'd re-found and I decided to call it a night – or day – and head back to the hostel. We still weren't tired, so kept ourselves amused by burying our friend in the sand on the beach when he fell asleep... probably the most fun I've had in a while.

But you know what they say about one man's meat being another man's poison (although a friend of mine has a rather unique theory that the real saying goes: 'One man's meat is another man's *poisson*', which he reckons would make far more sense, it being a continuation on the food theme and all that). Anyway, like everything gap-related, nightlife isn't a one-size-fits-all activity. What turns one person on ('I know, let's dance in a cage! Wearing leopard-print underpants! And blow a whistle!') will sound like slow torture to someone else. And the Full Moon Party is no exception. Here's Vix Carter's rather different take, from her gapyear.com diary:

On the twenty-third we went to the Full Moon Party on Koh Phangan, which was interesting to say the least. It was fun but I wouldn't go again! I think we were a bit disturbed by the number of old men there picking up the lady boys. Now I have seen some really convincing lady boys but the ones we witnessed were fairly manly and the strange thing was that the old men did not seem to notice! Oh well, good luck to them – I hope they had a good night.

TRAVELLER'S TOP TIP
Caroline North says keep something for 'best'

'I know it sounds ridiculous when you have to cram everything you need for your entire life into a bag the size of a pea, but you'd be amazed how big a confidence boost you get if you reserve one item for 'going out'. In my case it was a tiny crushed silk camisole top that took up no space at all but I only wore to go out at night. Even if I hadn't had a hot shower for three weeks, I could put that top on and still feel fantastic!'

Elsewhere in the world, nightlife provides a valuable insight into the inner culture of a given country (NB – memorise that phrase; believe me, it'll come in very handy during those hungover conversations with the folks back home). It's also the best way to try to get lucky with the local talent. Here's Stef Marianski's four-point plan of a night out, St Petersburg style, from his gapyear.com diary:

1. The Russians party through the night and into breakfast. It's common to see people come off the dance floor at six in

the morning and sit down to breakfast and coffee before carrying on!

2. The etiquette is different from England; it's always the girl who approaches the bloke. And most of them LOVE the English.

3. The popular clubs are vast, with at least six dance floors in one of the clubs we were in last night, plus a few bars.

4. Drinking goes on but no one really gets drunk. It's mostly all sober and any drinking takes place in a bar instead. There's no drunken moshing like a muppet. And incidentally, there's generally no drugs at all involved with clubbing.

In actual fact, our Stef seems to have been impressively determined to conduct his own one-man anthropological survey of the nightclubbing habits of various peoples around the globe. Here he is again in Beijing, China:

Finally arrived in Beijing yesterday morning and went straight out on the piss. Great place! Pity we only have three days here, I love this city. Not as cheap as Russia but at least the taxi drivers don't try to con you. Clubs are pretty hard core – finally, a place that plays hip hop instead of techno! We met a random German guy and a dude from our hostel and went to this place called Vics. Oh, and the ladies all love the English. Especially if you put on a posh accent ('How do you do? My name is Lord Stef and I have a country house').

Everywhere we go we are asked if we want to go to a good 'ladybar'... and they hassle you no end. The only guaranteed way to shake them off is to say: 'No, we want men!'

Nightlife, Thrills, Fun

Oh, and here he is in Japan, sampling the delights of the Tokyo club scene:

> The nightlife is great, and the Japanese are the most friendly people in the world and seem to love practising their English on Westerners! We didn't make any Japanese friends to go out with, though, because each in turn would get trolleyed and go home. Going out can be very cheap if you remember the following two facts: 1) The big nightlife areas like Roppongi and Shibuya are full of rich drunk businessmen who love to throw money about buying drinks and generally making idiots of themselves, and 2) Japanese people generally CAN'T hold their drinks – more than a couple and they're pretty plastered, so just a little bit off the beaten track you can find loads of clubs and bars offering all-you-can-drink nights.

Being a gay gapper always adds an interesting twist to the nightlife angle. Depending where you are in the world, gay bars and clubs might be underground and very difficult to penetrate or, as in Patong, you might have to be blind, deaf and extremely dumb to miss them. Justin Hurn, travelling with straight mate Lydia, conducted his own survey – purely in the interests of scientific research, of course (gapyear.com):

> Well, nightlife here is pretty interesting. You have hundreds and hundreds of bars with one thing in common: there are female prostitutes in them all. If you are a white guy with blond hair be prepared to have constant attention from the ladies! But for the gay scene here there are two streets of similar size to Old

Compton Street in London. There seems to be a Thai following for James Dean here as at least two of the bars are named after him...

It is quiet on the scene here since the tsunami but all the bars are very welcoming. If you are with a female they look at you like you shouldn't be there, but we found once they know you, everybody will speak to you – it's definitely got the community feel. At the end of the street there is a gay club open till 1 am which starts early with drag cabaret (well worth seeing for the comedy element of it). Then the DJ plays funky house until close – so you head round the corner where you have two straight clubs open till 3 am...

The best club here has to be SAFARI. The name says it all. It's set up in the forest-covered hills. You enter a gravel car park off the main road to be greeted by a loud bass line in the trees. Once you enter it's all open air set around a fair size lake with wooden footpaths running around. It's just like the Jennifer Lopez video 'Waiting for Tonight'.

THRILLS

TRAVELLER'S TOP TIP

Zac Preston says plan ahead for extreme sports:

'If you're the kind of person who's likely to do something mad like skydiving or bungee jumping, make sure your insurance covers it from the start. Most people decide to do things like that on the spur of the moment, but if something goes wrong and you're not insured, you'll end up paying massively for it. I met a guy who was travelling alone after his buddy blew his budget on brain scans after suffering headaches following a bungee jump. He ended up being fine, but so broke he had to cut short his trip.'

You'd think, wouldn't you, that a section devoted to people who choose to hurl themselves into mid-air from perfectly good, functioning planes or into ravines with ropes tied round their ankles would be a rather short section. Maybe even a joke section. Not so. Thrill-seeking has become a major part of many gap year itineraries, with intrepid gappers trying to outdo one another with tales of derring-do.

'When people come back from their gap years and show off their photos, it's the ones of them jumping from great heights or white water rafting that they get out first,' says gapyear.com's Tom Griffiths, who was himself first drawn to travelling by seeing pictures of his brother boom-netting (which involves being dragged along on a net by the side of a boat – but as that sounds, frankly, ridiculous, I accept there might be an element I've missed out).

'My best gap year moment came in Cairns,' Tom continues. 'I'd done my first bungee jump and I was bouncing back up and kind of sitting in mid-air and I let out this great big scream: "Yeah – this is what I've been waiting to do!"'

You've probably gathered that I'm not one of those who gets a buzz from being dragged behind a speeding boat attached to an outsized kite or launched up into the stratosphere via a giant catapult. Okay, I'll admit it. In theme parks and fairgrounds even the spinning tea cup ride gives me an adrenaline rush so intense I fear for the state of my heart. So I'm not the best person to talk about white water rafting, bungee jumping, skydiving or any of those other pursuits most gappers seem to consider 'fun'. Instead, I'll leave it up to the ex-gappers themselves to convey some of the excitement of extreme foolishness, I mean sports. For most gappers, Queenstown, New Zealand, seems to be a Mecca for all things extreme. Here's gapyear.com's Pete Kehoe:

Greetings from Queenstown! If you enjoy throwing yourself off bridges or canyons, body-boarding through grade four/five rapids and riding jet-boats through narrow gorges, this is the place for you!

Those of you who know me will know that I am not the greatest when it comes to heights. So it would come as no surprise when only Simon volunteered for the bungee jumping! As I type he is jumping from a perfectly good cable car with a 134 metre drop. Fool! I prefer the much more interesting concept of the canyon swing!

When we arrived at the swing, all you could see was a very, very big drop (102 metres) and a shed on a jetty over the cliff. The aim of the canyon swing is to jump, fall, run, flip off the end of the jetty and freefall for 60 metres, then complete a large arc when the ropes go taut! As I was terrified to say the least, I volunteered to go first! I chose the pin drop as my jump style. There are ten different styles to choose from – go to www.canyonswing.co.nz if you want to have a look!

The pin drop involved jumping off the edge sideways and experiencing speeds of 120 to 130 kph! As I fell all I could think was 'please let this rope hold'! If this wasn't enough I decided to take advantage of their $35 second jump! This time I did the 'gimp man goes to Hollywood'. This one involved me being suspended upside down over the canyon and then released and left to hurtle towards the ground headfirst at 150kph! It didn't help that the crew were saying things just as they released me like 'Wait – the harness is coming undone!' I have to apologise to anyone within a 50 km radius as the language was rather colourful! This was possibly one of the greatest things I have ever done. The adrenalin has only just started to slow down!

If you are in Queenstown I would recommend anyone to do this. The thrill of the ground rush and pulling out of the dive at the last moment was awesome!

TRAVELLER'S TOP TIP
Check the safety record, says Tom Griffiths:

When it comes to something like bungee jumping, you're literally putting your life in someone's hands, so we always advise people only to jump with the experts. Do your research beforehand – look the company up on the Internet or ask around to find personal recommendations. Of course I completely ignored my own advice recently and did a rap-jump (like abseiling but facing the other way) in Bath with a company I knew nothing about. This guy threw a rope over a cliff and said, 'Off you go, then.' It wasn't until I was halfway down that I even thought to question whether he was licensed. Not too bright!

Samantha Joly was another one who experienced first hand the joys of plummeting towards the New Zealand ground faster than a hobbit's adam's apple. Here's her Queensland gapyear.com diary entry:

So, the next morning, after not too much sleep, we headed up to the bungee centre. We decided that as we were in Queenstown we couldn't not do a bungee, and what was the point of doing a bungee if it wasn't going to be the very highest one (second highest in the world in fact)? So we signed in and were weighed and everything and then had to wait for half an hour before we were taken on a forty-minute four-by-four trip up to the Nevis site (driving up scary windy roads didn't help that much).

When we got up there, we put on our harnesses and were weighed again, and then I found out that I was going to be in the first group (ARGH!). So four of us went out in a very, very small cage to the cable car (trying desperately not to look down, and not succeeding.) Thankfully I wasn't first. That fell to John, who was scared of heights, and then went Sissy, and then me. Wow, I was so nervous, my legs were shaking. All the time I was sitting in the seat getting attached to the bungee cord I was breathing deeply trying to think of anything but jumping, but then also thinking about having to pull on the cord that would bring me up to a sitting position (second bounce) and bring me back to the cable car more comfortably than upside down. And then it was my go.

Walking to the edge was probably the scariest bit because your legs are so close together, you can't really walk, you have to shuffle along. I just thought, 'If I trip

and fall, I'm going to have no control over this at all.'
So there I was, at the edge, 200 metres above the
ground, not looking down. That's the trick, do NOT
look down, just look straight ahead. I was still
desperately trying to convince my stomach to retreat
back into my body when the bloke started counting
'three... two... one', and I jumped! I actually jumped!
There was no hesitation at all, I just did it. I knew that
if I didn't do it on my first go, I wouldn't do it at all, so
I just did it. And Jeezy Creezy, 8.4 seconds of freefall is
a bloody long time, let me tell you. What was weird,
though, is that I wasn't scared at all on that first fall. I
think my thoughts, from when I jumped, went from
'Oh my god!' to 'Oh, this is different'. Because it is – a
totally different feeling from anything you've ever felt.
Ever. It was such a shock that I forgot to scream!

Then, after 134 metres, the bungee very, very gently
bounces you back up, and you get to freefall all over
again. By that time I was desperately trying to find the
cord to pull me up to sitting position. I tugged and
tugged at it but it just wouldn't budge. So I ended up
having to be pulled back up to the cable car upside
down, which was pretty darn scary, I can tell you. When
they unclipped me from the bungee I was SO close to the
edge, I thought I was going to fall off and die! Seriously!

And then, suddenly, it was all over. I was alive! It was
the best feeling ever – having survived! After that, I
don't think I could have been scared of anything if I'd
tried. I was jumping around the cable car like there was
no tomorrow – actually stepping on the see-through
sections (which I was terrified of before the bungee).
Then on the way back over, I wasn't even phased about

going back in the cage over to the mainland. We were able to watch our DVDs on the screen before buying them (hilarious, you all have to see it!) and then we were back on the bus and back into Queenstown, and it was all over!

Honestly, I feel like I could do anything now. I'm totally up for another three goes... well, maybe...

Even gappers of previously sound mind who, like me, fail to see the entertainment value of feeling your insides exit your body, and return in not at all the order in which they left, can sometimes be seduced into believing that jumping off a small ledge into thin air might actually be a worthwhile use of time and money. Joe Bloomfield is one gapper who allowed himself to be swayed (gapyear.com) ...

The reason I decided to jump was that I watched a load of people doing the Kawarau Bridge bungee the day before, and there were quite a few people afraid to do it who just bit the bullet and leapt. I kind of realised I was being a bit of a girl about it by refusing and that it was all very safe, so I tried to sign up to the Nevis. No luck as it was all booked up, so I signed up for the Ledge.

When we got there, all the people I was with had booked 'The Thrillogy' which consists of three different bungees. They had all jumped Nevis earlier that day and were jumping the Ledge as the last of the three.

The Ledge differs from the other two as the bungee cord is attached to your waist rather than your feet, so you have a bit more freedom as to what you can do during the jump. The guys were all excitedly discussing what they were going to do and throwing all sorts of ideas into the mixer. Meanwhile, I stood there in nervous silence chewing my lip and trying not to regret the decision.

We were all grouped together in weight categories and one of the guys in my category (lardy) decided he wanted to film everyone else doing it, so we had to wait till last.

So there I stood, spectating in quiet horror as people did forward somersaults off the ledge, leapt off and turned mid-air to shoot at the camera à la *The Matrix*, did backflips, backsprings and cartwheels. One guy had even gone to the trouble of buying himself a Buzz Lightyear mask from the two-buck shop just so he could shout 'To infinity, and beyond!' before leaping off.

Finally my time came. I ran up to the ledge at full pelt, having decided to do a somersault. But one step before the edge my subconscious sense of reason kicked in and rather than leaping I kind of fell forwards off the edge. I still just about managed a somersault, but let's just say I wouldn't have got many points in the form category if bungee jumping were an Olympic sport.

Once the cord sprang me back up again I had a chance to look round. The views were awesome. The moon had just risen over the Remarkables (a mountain range so called because in the words of John Motson they are 'quite remarkable') and the reflection was shimmering across the lake towards me. Although the ledge is only a 47 metre bungee, it's actually situated 400 metres up a hill and you have to get a cable car to get to it, so I got to look out over the lights of Queenstown as well.

To round it off, I think I should point out that skydiving and bungee jumping weren't even on my list of 'Things to Do'. In fact, they were on my 'Things to Never, Ever, Ever Do in a Million Years For the Sweet

Love of God' list. I think I surprised quite a few people with my change of heart on the bungee front.

I wouldn't like to give the idea that gap year thrills necessarily have to be anti-gravity related. After all, there's plenty of adrenaline-rushing to be got from, say, squishing yourself through an underwater tunnel the size of a sausage to get to an underwater cave or climbing sheer rock faces with the aid of just a toothpick (or whatever the technical term is) or swimming with sharks. Swimming with what? Here's Ian Taylor's gapyear.com diary:

'Oh, poo' doesn't quite describe the bolt of mortal panic that shot through my blood at that moment, but that's what I said and it came out all muffled because I had the snorkel in my mouth. In the pool of pale, murky light from a spotlight on the boat I saw what was quite clearly a shark. It was about 2 metres long. About as big as me, then.

Me and the German bloke next to me exchanged a look before he asked our guide if she was 100% certain that the shark wouldn't attack us. She turned with a reassuring smile and said, 'No.' Another quick exchange between the German and me. She misunderstood the question, surely. She couldn't possibly take me into the dark water knowing there was a man-eater around… A minute later and that's where we were, anyhow. I'd had a little trouble with my mask – no spit to clear it, y'see, just like Richard Dreyfuss in *Jaws*. Wait… useless comparison.

There were only two of us in the water because everyone else was farting around with their flippers. On the boat, some child of Satan was chanting 'Shark-bait! Shark-bait!' and the only other sound I was aware of was that of my own breath through the snorkel. It was desperate and heavy so there was no use trying to convince myself I wasn't petrified.

The bloody shark had disappeared and in the deep water around the boat, the only things I could see with my torch were ominous bubbles and my own scrawny white legs doing a fair impression of those shots in shark films – you know the ones, where a soon-to-be-eaten set of limbs are seen from the shark's point of view kicking maniacally at the surface.

Everyone else eventually joined us and, mercifully, we swam away. Not that it's terribly comforting being far from the boat in the dark, but at least it wasn't as deep here and I could see the bottom – and anything that swam between it and me. But then, of all the happy coincidences, my sorry excuse for a torch started to flicker and at intervals for the rest of the time in the sea, it plunged me into complete darkness and pitiful fear.

Ah, well. I made it and back on the ship I learned that these reef sharks aren't really that dangerous. Still, I could have used that information most productively about half an hour earlier. No question, though – this was the most exhilarating thing I've ever done.

Genuine adrenaline junkies can spend their entire gap year bungee jumping between one thrill and the next. If there's a wave, surf it; if there's a mountain, climb it; if there's a sand dune, go down it very fast on a small board, like Neil Jones in Peru (gapyear.com):

The main attraction is sandboarding. I did a tiny bit in Oz on the west coast, but these dunes were about five times the size. So we signed up for a dune buggy tour, all four of us. Think of the best rollercoaster you've ever been on, and this was a hell of lot better – zooming around the desert and up and then over near-vertical dunes. We were bouncing all over the place, sitting at the back having no clue what was going to happen next. Yeah, lots of fun. And getting driven to the top of dunes saved loads of time and effort. First time we all went down head first on our bellies. Then we all tried our hands at boarding and all but one guy with snowboarding experience fell over within half a metre. But gradually everyone started to be able to go for a couple of metres or more. So we did this for an hour or so at different dunes, all pretty big. Then we got taken to the monster dune.

Having seen everyone plod their way down a metre or so at a time and finally make it to the bottom, I set off. 'Very strange,' I was thinking to myself as, 5 metres after setting off, I'm still standing. Then 10 metres, 15 metres. 'Okay, this is very cool and very fast. Oh, and very scary.' Still standing upright after 30 metres, I was not thinking too much about how the hell I was going to stop, but more about how painful it was going to be. Then, like clockwork, over I went, tumbling again and again and again, each time banging my head and getting another mouthful of sand (note to self – close mouth next time). By all accounts it looked pretty spectacular from the bottom – an explosion of sand. And then I came to a stop – sand everywhere, a nice sandy paste in my mouth and a very painful neck. It took a while for my head to clear well enough to respond to the calls of 'You alright, Neil?' A painfully fun day. I still have sand in my ears now!

Chapter 14
MAKING THE MOST OF IT

Carpe diem – *'Seize the day'*
Horace, Odes I, xi

Here's a question for you. How many times has the phrase 'trip of a lifetime' cropped up over the course of this book?

a)   Never heard it before
b)   Once or twice maybe, but then I did doze off through most
        of the middle section
c)   Loads, and can you stop repeating yourself, please?

The correct answer of course is c) but the fact is, that this is one phrase that bears repeating. Your gap year is likely to be the greatest adventure of your life. Sure, you might eventually land a job that involves lots of travelling to far-flung destinations or you might earn enough for two or three foreign holidays a year, but you'll never again have the same sense of freedom, of not being answerable to anyone but yourself, of sheer limitless possibilities.

For what may be the only time in your life, and with only your budget to constrain you, you can go where you want, change your plans at a moment's notice, take risks, reinvent yourself. The opportunities are endless – and it's up to you to seize them with both hands, feet, ears, eyes and everything else you have. Because it's the adventures you don't plan that make for the most vivid of memories. Ex-gapper Amy Cox says:

> It sounds corny but the key to really making the most of a gap year is to open your mind – to new people and new ideas. We spend such a lot of time in this country worrying that the man next to us is carrying a bomb in his bag, or the teenager in the hoodie is going to mug us, that we become very unreceptive. Fear closes us off from making eye contact or getting too close, so we also cut ourselves off from the possibility that they might have something good to offer us.
>
> When you're away you have to really try to forget that kind of conditioning. Of course you've got to use common sense to stay safe, but don't assume everyone's out to harm you or rip you off. I did things on my gap year I'd never dream about doing at home – like meeting a couple on a bus in Guatamala and going to stay at their house for a few days, or letting the guy who rented out boats on the beach in Brazil take me back to his home village and show me around. But those experiences were more enriching than any of the organised tours.

Ask any returned gapper to talk you through their photos (remember that this is a rhetorical remark; I wouldn't for a moment suggest you actually do such a reckless, unhinged thing) and I'll bet they'll get most animated when talking about the ones that involved doing something spontaneous or impromptu: 'Here's me holding the sheep's head I've just picked out of my soup in that funny little place the guy in the Internet cafe recommended!' 'Here's me showing the taxi driver's grandma how I can turn my eyeballs inside out after he invited me home for dinner!'

Sixteen years after returning from her gap year, it's the spur of the moment decisions that Helen Woodward remembers most vividly:

- Hitching a ride in a helicopter in New Zealand with my two new Swedish friends, Eva and Monica. (We were actually picked up in a 'ute' but the guy was a crop sprayer and offered to take us up the coast in his helicopter – unbelievable!)
- Seeing Linford Christie get a gold medal for his 100 metre sprint at Mount Smart in Auckland – and my gran seeing me on TV sitting in the audience!
- Trekking in Northern Thailand and staying in houses on stilts with villagers every night – that was incredibly exciting and different from anything I'd ever done before.

The biggest and most empowering thing about my time away (when not working for periods) was waking up every morning and having NO ONE telling me what to do, how hard to work, where I ought to go that day, what I ought to be doing. I COULD DO EXACTLY WHAT I WANTED! Never before and never since have I felt quite so free and unrestricted. This for me was the real beauty of travelling – I went with the flow, changing my plans all the time, taking opportunities as they presented themselves.

Sometimes you have a split second to make a choice that can mean the difference between a mediocre experience and a life-changing one. This is exactly what happened to Sarah Cumming in South Africa when she decided on a whim to slip under the tape dividing 'Public' from 'Press' at a major event (gapyear.com).

Robben Island was last on my 'Things to Do in Cape Town' list as you had to book ahead your ticket for the 9 am boat (about R100 cheaper than the ones during the day), and I actually managed to get a place on the day when the Olympic Torch was going to be passed on by Nelson Mandela. The trip involves a (return) twenty-minute boat crossing to the island, a tour of the prison (where Mandela was kept for twenty-seven years of his life) by an ex-prisoner and a somewhat rushed tour of the island, which also takes you to possibly THE best viewpoint of Cape Town and Table Mountain.

Because of the Torch Relay Ceremony our tour actually got cut short, which meant that we got to see a part of the celebration along with the island and its 200-odd inhabitants. As we were waiting outside the Robben Island Museum (to get maybe a glimpse of Mandela himself or the torch), I somehow managed to sneak into the press area (barely separated by tape) to get a bit closer to the entrance. Then an official looking lady came outside and announced: 'The ceremony is starting – Mandela is making his speech. Press, inside!' I basically got pushed inside the museum with the official press – and I mean the Big Boys: BBC, CNN, you name it, they were there! I don't know how I got past security as I had no ID but I think my flashy SLR camera helped me with that. I stuck on the biggest zoom lens I had in my bag (which looked pathetic next to some of the gear that the pros had) and tried my best not to look lost.

I managed to get a couple of feet away from Nelson Mandela and was there for the whole speech and handover ceremony! Not only that, but afterwards when Mandela and the other important SA government officials were posing for pictures and being interviewed or making statements, I even got to shake Nelson Mandela's hand! Afterwards my hands were shaking so much I don't know how the pictures will turn out, but I used up a whole film so I'll definitely have some close-ups. It really was amazing and I still can't believe how close I got!

I realise I've probably somehow incriminated myself here but it's such an unbelievable story I want to make everyone jealous. I was on a high for the rest of the day and I still haven't got tired of telling the story. On the boat back (I obviously sneaked out and re-joined my tour before I got caught), I got a few 'Oh... so you're with the press now, are you?' looks – but they were just jealous!

LETTING GO OF THE FEAR FACTOR

With so much attention being paid at the moment to safety while on gap years, it's easy to fall into the mindset of seeing every stranger as a potential mugger, every unfamiliar situation as a possible ambush. This kind of defensive thinking can greatly diminish the scope of your gap year, but according to top life coach and motivational speaker Fiona Harrold, the greatest thing we have to fear is fear itself:

Never stop seeing your gap year as an adventure. If you go equipped with fear then two things are going to happen: 1) You'll make your time away so unpleasant for yourself that you might as well not have gone in the first place, and 2) You'll attract the very thing you fear. People who are very fearful are the ones who get robbed or mugged; they're not the ones who get offered a spare room in someone's house or a job teaching English to someone's kids. Go away with an open mind and an optimistic outlook and adventures will come to you.

You can spend months back home planning your trip with military precision, but what makes it special won't be the fact that your forty-five-minute plane-change at Dubai went like clockwork, or that the whale-watching tour you booked months ago matched up to its description on the website. Instead, the memories you'll treasure will be the ones you never expected – like finding that your arrival in a country coincides with a national celebration, as happened to Dhruti Shah:

We arrived in Vietnam the night of the Southeast Asia games, which were being hosted in the country, and whenever Vietnam won a game (which suspiciously was rather often), the entire city would congregate in the centre of Hanoi and embark on a motorcycle cascade lasting several hours whilst everybody shouted: 'Vietnam, Number One!' We were given flags and banners and people randomly took pictures of us. It was all very surreal. I didn't even like football before that night.

Sometimes you'll make a spur-of-the-moment decision that will be a real dud. You'll make a detour to that 'awesome' church to find it overrun with Japanese holidaymakers intent on videoing inanimate objects like 'the wall' or 'the window'. Or you'll seek out that 'brilliant' lagoon and find it reduced to a puddle by a season of drought. But just occasionally everything – weather, mood, season – will come together to form one unique, perfect moment. Here's Ewan Dinwiddie's description of his trip to Ayers Rock (gapyear.com):

Up to this point we'd had a fair few light showers, but nothing compared to what was in store for us late that afternoon. We were once again off to 'The Rock' for more base walking when the heavens opened. The following couple of hours I will never forget – we simply drove around in the pouring rain staring in amazement as hundreds of waterfalls appeared on the Rock. At one point I saw a lightning bolt hit the top of it. I simply can't describe how incredible it all was.

After a while we pulled up and a few of us ran to a small, permanent waterhole at the base of the Rock. The entire area was overflowing with water. The guide, despite previously having told us that we were not to swim here as it is a sacred Aboriginal site, couldn't resist and jumped in. We followed. After a while the others left to go back to the bus leaving me there alone in the pool to just look around and take it all in... swimming at the base of Uluru, in the middle of the desert as a waterfall poured down next to me. Absolutely amazing! I will never forget that moment. Then a German tour group arrived and I was told in no uncertain terms to exit the pool...! So no definitive

Uluru sunsets or sunrises, but that experience more than made up for it.

TRAVELLER'S TOP TIP

Tom Griffiths says common sense and safety nets make for great adventures...

The world's an amazing place, but it can also be a dangerous place – that's why you have to put safety nets in place before taking risks while travelling. If an opportunity comes up, ask yourself whether your gut feeling is to feel comfortable with it, then make sure there are people who know exactly where you are and who you're with. I hitchhiked across Canada when I was twenty-one. It was an amazing experience, but I took every precaution to minimise the risks – never getting stuck in a remote location, always making sure I checked out the car before getting in it. Take risks, get off the beaten track, but do it safely.

Great experiences don't have to involve amazing scenery or spectacular history. Sometimes it's just a question of doing something so completely and utterly 'different' that it reminds you all over again: 'This is really me! I'm here! I've done it!' Who'd have thought, for example, that taking a bath abroad could be such a novel experience? Here's Stef Marianski's gapyear.com diary:

Banya – the Russian bathhouses. This was especially good for us because they've shut off our hostel district's hot water for post-winter repairs. Anyway, you go in, strip off and go into the hottest sauna you can imagine until you can't take it anymore (in the sauna the Russians beat each other with leaves for some reason, looks painful), then get out and plunge straight into an icy pool.

I loved it except for the fact that it's full of fat, old, wrinkly, naked Russians who don't really like foreigners, especially as *banyas* are just for the super rich (a whopping two quid to get in), so we're kind of taking the piss by milking their currency.

By far the most extraordinary among all extraordinary gap year experiences occur when an opportunity to do something you've been desperate to do for years, but never managed to achieve at home, suddenly lands in your lap while you're, say, feeding your camel in the Sahara or shinnying up a palm tree in the Carribbean to hack off a fresh coconut. When Sarah Ford went to Ghana to do a placement that involved half teaching and half helping out on a local paper, she never in a million years imagined she'd end up working for the BBC. She explains what happened in her gapyear.com diary.

Well, if you read my last post you'll know that on a trip to Elmina Castle I met a crew filming for the CBBC programme *Xchange*. I gave the producer, Gilly, a call on Sunday night when I got home and sorted out going to help them the next day, bright and early.

I left the house before 6 am. That's early. There was also no traffic which meant I was even earlier than I needed to be. I hung out in the tro-tro station, got some breakfast and made my way to their hotel. Was rather nervous at this point. Didn't want to get in their way completely.

On the Monday we went to film in a school called the Jack and Jill School (I say we, I mean they, it's just easier). They started off by filming one of the girls doing an introduction to her class. I got the job of holding the monitor which meant I was at least a little bit useful rather than standing in the background doing nothing. I got to watch how it all worked, which was great.

At the end of the school day, while the weather was just about holding out, we went to film at Labadi beach. It was a piece to camera with Gemma, the presenter. After that, we had cocktails at the beach hotel. Very nice. I'd had a really good day and to make it better they asked me to go back the next day to help out.

Tuesday: I was teaching till nine so I made my way to the Jack and Jill School after that. That afternoon, I worked with a few of the children who were going to be filmed the next day reviewing different items. I took them to watch some music videos, play with a few toys and have a go on the PlayStation. I had a chat with them, asked them what they thought of each thing so that when they went in front of the camera they had an idea of what they would say. They were really great – had their own ideas and were really constructive.

That night the crew were invited to the house of the Head of the British Council for dinner. They wanted to take me along so I borrowed some clothes (had a hot shower – bliss) and had a gorgeous meal and attempted to do some schmoozing.

Thursday: the day the BBC crew go back to England.

Went to meet them about 8.30 to go to a church, the Action Chapel. Pretty sure it must be one of the richest churches in Ghana. Absolutely spectacular. There were a lot of people but it wasn't even half full. The noise was just amazing. To see it full must be mind blowing. I'm not religious but that moved me. There was just this force and enthusiasm to it that's like nothing I've ever seen in a church in England.

Later, we went back to the hotel, had lunch and did some voiceovers. Then they were done. That's a wrap. It was so weird. I've really loved hanging out with them this past week and it was such an amazing opportunity. They've said that they'll be able to offer me work experience in the summer and eventually there might even be a job for me, as a junior researcher. The cameraman, who's freelance, also said he might be able to get me work experience. I just need to email my CV when I get back.

This has been such a great opportunity and I'm still unsure how it all happened. I just don't want to mess it up as contacts are so important in the media. I've had a great week and learnt more than I think I even realise right now. Ghana is, at times, the strangest place.

Chapter 15
BACK TO REALITY

'We shall not cease from exploration
And the result of all our exploring
Will be to arrive where we started
And know the place for the first time.'
T S Eliot, Four Quartets

'If travel is searching, and home what's been found,
I'm not stopping, I'm going hunting.'
Bjork, 'Hunter'

There will come a moment, no matter how fantastic a time you're having, when thoughts start to turn to home. A week or so before the end of your trip, you'll start to look forward to:

1. The first cup of tea!
2. Sleeping in a bed with clean sheets!
3. A fully flushing loo! That you can sit on!
4. Impressing your mates with your tan and photos!
5. The first pint in your local!
6. Your mum's roast dinner!

7. The Sunday papers!
8. Wearing a jumper! (oh, the novelty!)
9. Having a long bath! With hot water! And no one banging on the door because you're taking too long!
10. Not being stared at in the local supermarket! Oh, and...
11. Being with your family!

You'll start playing out your triumphant return in your head. Won't everyone be pleased to see you? Will they notice you've lost half a stone? How will that Chinese character tattoo go down with Dad?

HOMECOMING

A truly great dramatic homecoming is one of the big pay-offs of a good gap year. It's the icing on the cake, the froth on the lager, the little ball of chewing gum at the bottom of a Screwball ice cream. Plan it right and you and your family will be dining off that story for years to come ('Grandma, tell us again about the time Dad got himself delivered home in a parcel!').

Timing a homecoming to coincide with a memorable family event like a birthday or wedding makes it even more likely that you'll come back with a bang rather than a whimper (word of advice: best not to pop up unexpectedly at a funeral – there are occasions where it doesn't do to upstage the guest of honour). Tom Garrett opted for the classic Mum's Birthday Homecoming Scenario. Here's his gapyear.com diary:

> Knowing that I was to return a little early allowed me to fly back to England on my mum's fiftieth birthday. She knew nothing about it – nobody did. I needed to keep it all quiet because I needed to be able to just walk in and surprise Mum. So that was the plan. And it went

well. Mum was sad that I wasn't going to be there for her celebration meal, so it was going to make my re-entry shock a little more interesting.

I will never forget the moment. I said hello to my sister and was told that I was to walk in with the birthday cake while everyone was singing 'Happy Birthday'. Sounds easy. The reaction was priceless. Mum looked at me and then had to do a double take. Then she dropped her spoon and screamed and then started crying. It all went very well and made my return a great day.

Sometimes, however cleverly you plan your homecoming, it just doesn't go quite as you'd imagined. Joe Bloomfield orchestrated his triumphant return with a director's eye for the dramatic – if only his supporting actors had bothered to learn their parts (gapyear.com):

On 17 December I was due to fly home. Not that my family knew that, of course. I had originally been booked to fly home on 7 December, but since I'd come away, my friends and ex-housemates Mike and Elaine had organised a trip of their own and were due to fly in to Bangkok on the 9th, so I put my flight home back by ten days so that I could stay out to see them. However, I told the folks I'd postponed it for a month, and would be home on 7 January. In the meantime I had a suit fitted and met up with Mike and Elaine. After a couple of days chilling with them on Koh Samet, we got back to Bangkok.

On 16 December I picked up my suit, put it on, packed my bag and headed to the airport, with the plan of turning up in Ipswich wearing my suit and surprising the family by coming home for Christmas.

After a long flight home, and a nice easy train journey, I rolled up in a taxi down the hill from my house. My plan was to phone them, tell them I was calling from Bangkok to wish them a happy Christmas, because we were going to be spending it on an island and I didn't know if I'd be able to phone from there, and while I was on the phone to them, I'd let myself in and stroll in through the door.

I tried to phone and nobody picked up. Balls. I strolled up the hill and Dad was talking to the neighbour over the front wall. I called out to him and he turned to look at me with a frown of confusion on his face. The seconds ticked by as I smiled at him. After about ten or fifteen seconds, literally, his eyebrows raised as he worked out who I was. 'Joe!' he called, and after another extended pause, 'What the bloody hell are you doing home?'

We went inside and Oz, our pet dog, didn't have the same trouble recognising me. I had to do a few deft sidesteps to stop him ruining my new threads by jumping up at me.

Over a superb cup of tea (one of the main things I've missed) Dad told me the reason it'd taken him so long to work out it was me. He'd apparently seen the suit and the long dark overcoat and immediately thought, 'Oh no, it's the bloody Mormons come to preach at me.' Charming. He didn't even recognise his own son!

Later on my mum and sister came in. They both looked at me with the same confused expression, although they were both a bit quicker on the uptake than the old man.

After eight months away, visiting all the places I've visited and seeing all the things I've seen, I can now fully confirm the old proverb. There is officially No Place Like Home. However, ask me in a few weeks and I may well have itchy feet again...

The truth is that most gappers spend an inordinately long time towards the end of their trip planning how they're going to arrive home. And you know the great thing about a Homecoming Fantasy? Most, if not all of it, will come true exactly as you thought. Everyone will make a fuss of you, that first cup of tea will taste better than you ever thought, and wearing a jumper feels just so *cosy*. And this feeling of euphoria will last – ooh, easily until the second cup of tea. Maybe even the third.

COME-DOWN

But then another emotion will start creeping in. Discontent. 'So what's so great about being able to sit down while you pee?' you'll ask yourself. Was your local always so tacky? Aren't jumpers itchy?

You'll notice your tan has faded and you've regained that half a stone with the first roast dinner. Worst of all, after the initial excitement has worn off, your friends aren't really interested in hearing that funny story about how you found an iguana in your hammock, and tend to suddenly remember something pressing to do as soon as you whip out your stack of photos of sunsets over beaches.

For Sarah Cumming, who'd survived the 2004 tsunami and then gone back to help with the rescue effort before resuming her ambitious round-the-world trip, the post-travel blues hit harder than most, as her gapyear.com diary entry shows:

Oh, Blighty... I can't believe I'm writing this. For the last eighteen months I've been reading emails from other travellers returning to England and I never imagined it would get to the date when I had to write those words: 'I'm back in Blighty'. I don't think anyone else did either. I kept receiving emails from friends saying, 'Are you coming home ever? You're not, are you?' Well, I've been back in Blighty for five days now.

When I landed at Heathrow the American couple next to me on the plane asked me if I was excited to be back home, and I just stared out of the window and mumbled something about the grey colour of the sky. 'Oh, but you're used to it,' they replied. Grey, grey, grey, grey.

So now I've got over the grey and feel like I'm living in a palace with a comfortable bed, a toilet that you can sit on and, most importantly, HOT WATER! It's actually sunny today.

Nothing has changed. I didn't expect it to but I'm still surprised that nothing has changed. Same ads on TV, same unused bubble bath giftset in the cupboard. It's just like I went on holiday for a week.

Speaking of holidays, I'm already fed up of people saying that I've been on holiday for a year and now it's time to get back to reality. Come on, travellers, back me up here, it's not all holiday, is it? You call having no money to buy food, a wooden bed with no mattress, no hot water for twelve months and no shower, only a bucket for three months, a holiday?

And as for reality, I've had numerous conversations with people about this one – am I back in reality now, or have I just come from reality? My conclusion is that everyone has their own reality and in reality, there is no reality.

TRAVELLER'S TOP TIP

Time your return properly, advises Jane Yettram:

I think we came back at the worst time. We came back on Christmas Eve – so, great fun, lots of parties, friends, family for a week or so. Then a crash landing. London in January. Bleak, grey, cold and those dark months stretching ahead endlessly. My advice? Come back in the spring, after the clocks have gone forward. Daffodils, blossom, light evenings and the prospect of summer will make coming home feel better.

Note that bit where Sarah talks about nothing having changed, because that will become what is called a recurring theme. When you go off travelling or volunteering, even if you're away for only four months, it can be life-transforming. At the very least you come back with your horizons expanded like a panorama TV screen and your viewpoints changed on so many things. But see, here's the weird thing – four, six, even twelve months at home isn't so very long and, really, pretty much everything stays the same. So your friend Molly dyed her hair blonde. And Noah dumped Jessie for Katie, who then left him for the bloke in the mobile phone shop. But really, that's about it. Generally, people still live in the same houses, still drive the same cars, still work at the same jobs. It's like those films where someone goes off time travelling for a few decades or centuries and comes back yelling 'I'm back, did you miss me?' only to find that in real time, only minutes have passed and could they get a move on because they're late for their tea.

When my family and I got back from living in Catalonia for a year, I was amazed at the number of people I bumped into in our home town who'd say things like: 'Ooh, you look brown. Have you been on holiday?' Holiday! A year abroad with three children and all the ups and downs and adventures that entails, and as far as most people were concerned we might just as well have been on a fortnight's vacation in Lanzarote.

Tom Griffiths knows all about how frustrating this lack of acknowledgement of the *hugeness* of your gap year experience can be.

The time away goes by so quickly. You're bursting to talk about it. But nothing has changed for the people you left behind. It's called reverse culture shock – that period that lasts for up to a month where you feel completely spaced out. You just can't get to grips with the fact that nothing at home has changed but you've changed immensely, even if you've only been away a few months.

You'll see people in different ways because of the experience you've had. Maybe someone you always thought was quite cool will actually seem a bit shallow now. You reassess everything and everyone.

BEATING POST GAP YEAR BLUES

Jo Ash is UK Marketing and PR Officer for GAP Activity Projects. She also took a gap year in 1998, teaching in a New Zealand school and travelling around New Zealand, Australia, Fiji and America. Here's her advice on filling the travelling void:

A gap year is a brilliant, life-changing opportunity to see a bit of the world, gain life experience and develop your skill set, so what's the down side to it?

The answer to this is obvious... coming home! Take it from me, a returned gapper, the gap year experience will stay with you long after you return and here is how to beat the blues once the experience is over.

For the students among you – this is probably the easiest transition. Strange as it may sound, going back to study is actually relatively easy. Okay, it may take a while to get your brain back into gear but a gap year actually can help focus you on what you hope to achieve in your future. The cultural experiences and a constructive volunteering placement where you make a worthwhile contribution to those who need it will often make you more grateful for the opportunity of studying. Living away from home is also comparatively easy once you have survived living on the other side of the world, living and working in a different country – you will become well trained in being self sufficient and independent.

From the people I have spoken to, going back to work can be slightly trickier and is often affected by a range of factors. These factors include what you did while you were away, whether you travelled or completed voluntary work, how long you went for and what you were doing before you left.

Everyone is different and has different reasons for taking a career break and going on a gap year. Some decide to take a year out for life experience, to deal with the travel bug, see a bit of the world, and plan to return to their life once it is completed. Others take a gap year from work to find or change direction and this reason can have a big impact on settling back into life back home. It may be that your gap year teaching Tibetan monks in India or working in an orphanage has inspired you to change career direction and you embrace this once you're back, or it could leave you feeling discontented with your current life. The important thing to remember is that while most of us feel refreshed after going back to work after a holiday, the act of going back to work after a gap year is very different.

Whatever your reason for taking a gap year, it is important not to lose sight of it when you return. Often the act of travelling and living in another culture forces us to step outside our comfort zone, and be more confident and reflective. If you went away to find a new lease of life or a new career, use the experiences you have had on your year out to inspire you.

Financially, the return home after a gap year can be somewhat disheartening. After all the hard slog working, saving and fundraising, most people return from their gap years with stacks of memories, experiences, photographs and tales but minus any cash. No matter how well you have budgeted, once you are on a gap year you will want to take advantage of every amazing opportunity available to you. So returning home often equates with being skint. For the students out there, this is about to become a way of living (sorry, guys, but trust me, I spent four years studying...). However, the important thing for everyone to remember is that this won't last forever. Just as the experience was budgeted and saved for, the same can be done to rectify your financial situation on your return. Look at ways of saving money, make sure you're earning an income, and start to build up your finances again!

Ian Taylor is another one who experienced the Time Standing Still phenomenon when he got back from his travels, as he recounts in his gapyear.com diary:

It's been great showing off our photos and telling stories but nothing here has changed. I don't know why, but I expected to come back and find something different. Everything's frighteningly familiar and just as we left it. And although that's kind of a comfort – we were ready to come back, it's been really intense – it's almost as if we haven't been anywhere!

Except that we have, of course. We've been bloody miles. We were away for three months, which might be shorter than a lot of people's trips, but we didn't have to work at all and we saw an incredible amount of stuff. It was a bit whistle-stop – we didn't stay anywhere for more than five days – but without question, it was the most satisfying thing I've ever done.

When you've done something so mind-bogglingly amazing as take a gap year and seen the world, or at least some of it, what's the first thing you're going to want to do when you come home? That's right, you're going to want to talk about it. At length. To everybody. And it can come as a crushing disappointment to find that, actually, they're not really that interested.

After our Spanish year out, friends or other parents at the school gate would say, 'Wow, a year in Spain! What was that like? Amazing, hey?' But if I did anything more than nod my head and agree that, yes, 'amazing' more or less summed it up, they'd make that expression any returning gapper had better get very used to seeing. This is how it goes:

1. The eyes lose focus and take on a sort of glassy appearance or else dart around wildly trying to find some – any – distraction.
2. The lips draw back into a tight smile that says: 'I'm not actually listening to a word you're saying but if I must stand here, I might as well give my facial muscles a work-out while I'm doing it.'
3. The body weight shifts from one foot to the other as, like a sprinter before a race, they restlessly prepare for flight.

If you see this look, the best thing you can do is accept defeat gracefully. You have lost your audience. And whatever you do, don't try to win them back with increasingly extreme traveller's tales – 'Oh, but I haven't told you the one about the poisonous snake in the washbag, have I?' or 'Just wait until you hear what Josh and I got up to on the Inca Trail!' Watch my lips: they're not interested. They'll never be interested. They don't want to see your pictures, they don't want to hear your stories. They're not interested in learning why George ('Yes, you *do* remember him. Heather's friend, we bumped into him at a youth hostel just outside Rio') was such a great person to have around that time you had to spend thirteen hours at a bus stop in southern Mexico. All they want, really, is for you to smile and say, 'Yeah, it was great, thanks. Glad to be back, though.' And that will do very nicely, thank you very much.

When Harriet Chambers emailed me giving me permission to use parts of her gapyear.com diary in this book, she included a long update on her time abroad, then added an apology for having written me an 'essay':

> The thing, of course, is that when you get back no one really wants to hear about it, so when given the opportunity I think I tend to go on for hours. This seems to be the case with so many people I know who've been on gap years. Only other people who've done similar things seem to want to listen to you go on for hours about Vietnam or Malaysia!

You can't blame people. I mean, suppose your mate who's really into, say, civil engineering, goes out and gets his dream job building bridges. It's fantastic for him, right? It's life changing. He spends ten hours a day doing it, often more, so it totally consumes his life. But when you meet him for a pint on a Saturday evening and say, 'How's the job going?', do you really want him to launch into a full-scale detailed description of his working day with additional breakdown of the construction schedule of your average suspension bridge? Or do you want him to say, 'Yeah, it's great, thanks. Do you know whether Chelsea won their match this afternoon?' Tom Griffiths says:

The only people you'll be able to talk about your gap year to are other people who've done it themselves. My mates made it really clear they were bored stiff with my travellers' tales after I came back from my gap years. But I still found it hard to stop myself. We'd be in the pub watching the footie and they'd say, 'Wow, this is so exciting' and I'd say, 'Call this exciting! When I was in Oz...' but I'd never get a chance to finish what I was going to say because they'd either shout me down, yawn loudly or just walk off.

TRAVELLER'S TOP TIP

Rupert Mellor suggests that maybe travel can be what you do, rather than what you did...

Once the fun of seeing friends and family again fades, life 'back home' can seem a bit underwhelming. Chances are you did a lot when you were travelling, and your days felt packed with fresh, stimulating experiences. Keep yourself busy when you get home, and treat yourself to the kind of variety you got used to on your trip. And if the travel bug won't let you go, maybe you've found out that you're destined to work abroad, or in the travel industry, or as a travel writer, or as an eco-tourism pioneer.

TS Eliot once said 'human beings cannot bear very much reality' but actually, human beings can bear an awful lot of their own reality; it's other people's that they find mind-numbingly boring. But if you're disappointed at the way your nearest and dearest fail to be enthralled by your tales of exploration and adventure, that feeling can only be compounded by the heartless attitude shown by those in positions of authority over you like, say, bank managers or potential employers. Because when you return from your gap year, you're likely to have all these things: a) a tan, b) diarrhoea (you didn't think we'd get through a whole chapter without mentioning it, did you?), and c) a humungous overdraft.

The first two, a) and b), will soon disappear, but sadly c) is not so easy to get rid of. So, not only are you facing the come-down of being back home in the first place, you're also about to experience the depressing double whammy of being back home AND stony broke. Andy Frazer-Jones' post-return gapyear.com diary entry was written a couple of days after he jetted back from New Zealand:

> Since then I have met up with most of my friends and family, but when I look back at the photos I wish I was still out there. I am stuck with the realisation that it is time to get a job and pay off those ever-increasing debts. I am currently in the process of printing off my photos and sorting out the video footage I took of about nine months – a long, difficult job. As far as the job hunting goes, I am looking into graduate jobs and hope to nail a place next year. Then the big bucks can roll in and I can start planning another trip.

But before you start ripping up all the travel timetables and taking that stack of overdue Lonely Planet guides back to the library, convinced this whole gap year thing is more hassle than it's worth, there's another, more positive side to post-gap year blues. Sometimes the shock of coming back, combined with the sum of all you've learned while away, can jolt you out of your preconceived notions of what you want to do with your life and onto a whole new course altogether, which is exactly what happened to Dhruti Shah:

> Coming back was the worst bit. I returned home in February and had to go about finding employment. I was jobless for a month – and extremely depressed because I missed travelling and meeting new people. I then got a well-paid temping job, but I'd already decided while I was abroad that I wanted to make my dream of being a journalist a reality, so I started applying for graduate schemes and MAs. I also wrote about my trip for a few travel websites. I kept in mind how much fun I had had travelling and the skills I had learned. I worked for a travel magazine that sent me on an all-expenses-paid trip to Crimea, and then I got a bursary from a media group that trained me up and gave me a job on a local newspaper in London. All this because I decided to stave off the post-travelling blues by distracting myself...

The thing to remember about Post Gap Year Come-down is that it will pass. And that, though you may temporarily find yourself having dropped a couple of places down the food chain from your contemporaries who took the path of least resistance and went straight into a job or university course, in the long run you'll soon regain lost ground. Most probably you'll come out ahead, because a gap year allows you invaluable time out to reassess your priorities and work out where you really want your life to go – something your more sensible peers may not discover until their Mid-life Crisis, and by then it'll be too late. Travel presenter Sankha Guha's time away has made him truly value his home life: 'Back to reality? Love it. Being home is a holiday – I love my kids, my bed, my fridge, my guitars… my space in the centre of a whirling world.'

Helen Woodward didn't take her gap year until the relatively late age of twenty-seven, but she still credits it with giving her the confidence to start a whole new life when she got back.

I don't know about other people but when I got back I felt like I was capable of doing anything! All my old inhibitions seemed to have blown away. I was absolutely full of it. This feeling lasted a while but reality eventually crept back in. I had to find work and get on with my life.

I did not, as it turned out, make any massive career change as a result of my experiences. I did, however, manage to land a good job, move to a new part of the country and start a new chapter in my life. After being over the other side of the world, meeting new people and new challenges every day, this was a piece of cake.

I kept my filthy old rucksack, by the way – as a memento. I still look at it longingly when I open the cupboard. I still have itchy feet but am married and in the rat race now. It will never again be so easy to do what I did when I was twenty-seven.

WARNING: LESSONS TO FORGET!

Author Stuart Ferris says, 'Travel teaches valuable lessons about what's really important in life, how small and precious the world is, and how Western society is unnatural and unhealthy to the core. It's essential to forget these lessons the instant you return so that you don't turn into a hippy.'

Once you've got past the Back-to-Reality Blues, you'll be able to work out the lasting legacy of your gap year. And if that sounds rather pompous, it probably is. But it's undoubtedly true too. A gap year might leave you feeling fulfilled, it might leave you feeling frustrated. You might have got the travel bug out of your system and be content to settle down, or you might have been left with seriously itchy feet. But however it affects you, a gap year will never ever leave you feeling indifferent. You'll have laughed, you'll have cried, you'll have seen drunken sunsets and jet-lagged sunrises. You'll have met people you were glad to lose and people who'll be your friends for life. You'll have had moments of exhaustion and moments when you felt like you could conquer the world. And experiences like that leave their mark. You'll come back altered – and now is the time when you gingerly, like a recovering patient inspecting his wounds, try to find out how. Tom Garrett isn't the only gapper to find his experience left him with a whole new philosophy on life (gapyear.com):

> Today I unpacked my rucksack for the last time. Instead of laying it all out ready to repack, I threw stuff away and put other bits in for a wash. My rucksack is now

looking very tired and lies beneath my bed in its well-earned resting place. While I sat on my bed it hit me. For the first time, in a long time, it hit me. Bang. I smile and close my eyes and I am back on the beach, back in Vietnam or back in Oz. I am wherever I want to be now, whenever I want to be there. Because that's the gift that travel gives you. Unforgettable memories that you can return to forever... When I have a bad day now I think of those days on Fraser Island, skydives with Al, pick-up trucks in Cambodia, and my mates all across the globe.

So it is done. What can I say? What have I got out of all this? Where now? So many questions...

Backpacking is travel in a bubble. Safely bouncing from one place to the next. At the end of it all it's very easy to let that bubble burst. It causes you to fall back to earth with a thud. I just don't think that bubble ever has to burst. Sure, it's going to lose some air and float back down to the ground once in a while, but it should never burst.

Look at it this way. Life at home sucks. Or so it would seem. But that's merely an illusion brought on by a time of such independence and joy. Non-stop fun and freedom makes jobs, houses and kids look like prison sentences. But life, however you see it, is one big backpacking adventure. You just get to stay in one place for longer. You get to unpack your bag and work for longer. But the principles stay the same. You choose what you do with your life. You.

One thing that I have learnt from many of my friends on the road is that if you can extract and use the one recoverable positive from all the irrecoverable negatives that surround us, you have a great quality. So, go about life with a smile and a wave and treat all that comes your way as a new adventure. I know I will take that with me through the years and I know now that life owes me nothing. It merely gives me a chance to find my happiness.

I wish you all the very best. Live out your dreams, and be who you want to be even if you can't be what you want to be.

That's the thing about gap years, they make philosophers and poets out of us all. Because that stuff is inside all of us all the time – it just takes a time off and horizon broadening to let it out. And whether you pick up your rucksack again, dust it down and head back out into the world, or just frame your favourite memories and prop them up on your desk at your new job so you can be reminded of them while you get on with your life back home, your mind-frame will always be subtly altered because of having done Something Different.

Zoe Jeanes, who got back from her gap year in 2004, even wrote a poem about it, called 'When the World Was Mine'...

I sit at my desk and remember,
About a time when the world was mine.
I reminisce about my travels,
And the endless good times.

I think about my adventures,
The talk, the laugh, the sorrow.
It was completely amazing,
But I'm ready for tomorrow.

Back To Reality

It seems so long ago,
Yet still like yesterday.
But I know these memories,
Are in my mind to stay.

I saw so many places,
Sydney, Bangkok, Queenstown.
And when I remember these sights,
They never make me frown.

I think of the friends I made,
Bonds never to be broken.
I think of each and every person,
Of which I've often spoken.

I know in my heart,
My travelling stays with my forever.
And if I'm feeling down,
I can call on it whenever.
If the work gets hard,
Or I feel I don't have time.
I'll sit at my desk and remember,
About when the world was mine.

Chapter 16
TRAVELLERS' CASEBOOKS

CASEBOOK ONE: JOHN LAWLER, GHANA
John Lawler, 31, Newcastle
'My gap year started with falling down a drain...'

Before I went out to Ghana, I worried like everyone does about all the things that could possibly go wrong. 'One thing that I must never, ever do,' I promised myself, 'is to get ill and end up in an African hospital.' I'd seen all the TV footage. I'd heard all the horror stories about the lack of beds and dirty syringes.

So you can imagine how delighted I was when, within a couple of hours of getting off the plane, I fell down a storm drain in the street, snapped my ankle and spent my first night in Africa in a hospital bed being injected with painkillers. But then, if I hadn't had to spend the next few weeks limping around on crutches, maybe I wouldn't have made such an impression on the people of Shia. And if I hadn't made such an impression, I probably wouldn't now be Chief Togbe Mottey the First. The First Golden Rule of Gap Years: Don't make any rash promises!

Like most good things, my gap year came about largely by accident. I'd just finished my second year of an Environmental and Ecological Engineering course at Newcastle University and was informed in no uncertain terms that as there was no socialising module to the course, I was spectacularly underachieving. In effect, I was asked to leave the course. So I suppose it didn't technically start off as a gap year, more of a gap life. It wasn't until I went to Africa that I learned to appreciate the education I'd taken for granted and begged to be allowed back onto the course.

But all that was a long way off that summer in 1997 when I packed up all my university text books and started wondering what to do with the rest of my life. There's nothing like setting yourself a steady, sensible goal, so I immediately decided to apply for a visa to go and shear sheep in New Zealand with my friend Ross. We knew we'd need a fair bit of money for this, so I got a job working for Directory Enquiries. As I was living at home in Newcastle, I managed to save up loads of cash, but six weeks before we were due to fly off, Ross's mum suggested that perhaps we should be doing something a bit more, well, worthwhile with our time off. Like volunteering to teach out in Ghana.

I have to say, it's not something that had ever crossed my mind before, but once it was suggested I began to see the appeal. There was a guy from Kenya on my university course and I'd always loved hearing him talk about Africa. Plus I knew my CV, with its uncompleted university degree, was a bit of a disaster. I needed to be able to put something constructive down there – something more than backpacking around Thailand. And, of course, I had that whole Bob Geldolf Live Aid thing in my head. Of course, I thought. Ghana, I thought. Why hadn't I thought of it before?

In January 1998, I flew out to Ghana to meet up with Ross who'd flown out the week before. We'd signed up with a company that placed us in schools in the Ghanaian capital,

Accra. Everything was planned down to the last detail. What could possibly go wrong?

Right after coming off the plane, I decided to go for a walk. There were no pavements in that part of Accra but plenty of storm drains – one of which I managed to fall down. My ankle bone gave a sickening snap as it broke in two. Luckily Ross was already acquainted with the hospital, having gone there earlier in the week with someone who needed their appendix out. With me groaning in agony, we flagged down a taxi to take me to the hospital, which would be my home for the night. It wasn't quite how I'd envisaged passing my first evening in Africa!

I left the hospital the next day on crutches. But the plaster on my leg wasn't the only thing that put a damper on my first weeks in Ghana. I was also disillusioned with my teaching placement. I'd been placed at a well-off school in the capital, teaching A-Level geography (a subject I myself had not even done at GCSE level). Surely there was somewhere else I could make more of a difference?

Some time during those first weeks in Accra, I got talking to a group of volunteers who'd just got back from travelling around the country. They told me about a village they'd visited called Shia, up near one of the border posts, which was desperately under-resourced and in need of outside help in setting up a secondary school. Now that sounded a lot more like it.

I decided to quit my placement and go to find Shia – several hours' bus ride away – to offer my services in whichever way was needed. The elders of the village still talk about the day the Westerner on crutches arrived offering to help. They must have wondered whether I'd be helping them, or the other way round!

I stayed in Shia for four months, and right from the start I knew this was where I wanted to be. It's a beautiful place, up in the hills, reached by untarmacked dirt roads. Although malnutrition among the 2,000 or so villagers isn't as bad there as in the north of the country, there's still a huge need for monetary aid, particularly in terms of education. Schooling is relatively expensive in Ghana – £5 to £10 a term – not much but if you consider that a teacher might get £10 to £20 a month, it's a huge chunk out of a family's budget.

During my four months in Shia, I helped set up the secondary school and also went back to Accra to recruit more volunteers to come to the village and lend a hand. My hard work and commitment didn't go unnoticed. A week before I was due to fly back to the UK, I was driving around Accra with a village elder by the name of Justice when he announced he had something to ask me. Would I like to join the five existing chiefs of the honourary council as Chief of Development? It was an incredible feeling, a real 'wow factor'. Me – a Geordie lad on his first proper time away from home, being invited to become an African chief? It was unbelievable.

Justice explained that the other elders knew I'd formed a strong bond with the community and that I'd be back – hopefully bringing more people to visit. I was the first European who'd actually stayed and lived in the village. 'We saw this man appearing on crutches with a cast on his foot and thought, "What is this?"' Justice chuckled. He also explained that this was an honourary title. I'd be expected to go back once a year to get involved with various projects, including trying to find enough local employment for young people to stop them having to leave for the capital. The chief enstoolment ceremony would be in October. Would I come?

Well, how can you refuse an offer like that? When I got back to the UK and begged my way back onto the course, the first thing I had to do was ask for a week off. What for? Er, so that I can be made Chief Togbe Mottey I (which means 'chief pioneering pathfinder through the forest'). Luckily for me, the university recognised the benefits of one of their students becoming a Ghanaian chief and so it was that on 28 October 1998, my birthday in fact, I flew out to Ghana for a second time, accompanied by my mum and two of my sisters, to take up my new life as a minor royal.

It was the first time my mum had ever left the UK and she had no idea what to expect. On the flight out, one of my sisters asked my mum how much money she was taking with her. 'Five pounds,' came the reply, 'That'll be enough for a week in Africa, won't it?'.

There was a big welcome waiting for us in Shia. My sisters were made honourary princesses for the day. They were absolutely thrilled, but I was a nervous wreck. I knew I was going to have to recite the oath of allegiance in Ewe, the local language, in front of at least 2,000 people! I was handed it to learn the day before the ceremony, and had spent the entire day muttering it under my breath.

The day of the actual ceremony, I was sat on a throne on the stage, as were my mum and sisters, all of us fanned by village people as we sat in the sweltering African heat. I was fetchingly attired in a Ghanaian toga, teamed with a crown, sash and huge flip-flops. Oh, and they tied a string of beads around my arm and smothered me in talcum powder. Good look.

It was a huge cultural shebang. Even the Ghanaian TV cameras were there. In all the photos and TV footage, I look awful. So stressed and nervous. I hated the attention – hated every minute of it, really, until after my speech was done and I could relax.

The whole thing took eight hours. There were speeches and then dancing and singing, and then afterwards, a massive party. The next day there was a football match where friends and family played against the village team.

The whole occasion was overwhelming, really. Of course, my mum and sisters thought it was great. If you talk to my mum, she'll tell you how proud she was, and my sisters still go on about it now. I think it really opened their eyes. My mum had never seen relative poverty like that before, and it was a big thing for her to see what little the kids there have, and to know that I'm trying to help them.

During my final year at Newcastle University, I set up the MAD society – which stands for Mottey Africa Development. It was a project whereby I took seventeen Newcastle University students to Ghana to help out in the village. We built two classrooms for the secondary school and another two for the primary school. Then after I graduated, I set up Madventurer in January 2000. I wanted to set up a travel organisation that combined gap year placements with overland tours around Africa.

Since then, we've run projects to bring electricity to the village, and rebuilt and renovated every school in Shia, plus built assorted clinics and drainage systems. And now we've moved our attentions to other needy villages throughout the region and indeed throughout the world – we're running projects in rural communities in Africa, South America, Asia and the South Pacific. We're even involved in conservation expeditions to Antarctica.

A couple of years ago, the elders said to me, 'It's time you had your own place, Togbe.' So now I'm working on building my own house there, on the acre of land I was given when I became a chief.

I got married in the summer of 2006 to Elaine, or to use her full title, Mama Ama Wu Sika (which means 'people are more important than gold'). As I'm enstooled as chief, Elaine – who'd never been to Africa before – became Queen, making us Ghana's first white royal couple.

Because Elaine had never been to Ghana, she had to be inspected by the Shia dignitaries beforehand to make sure she was fit to be Queen. So a month before the wedding, the Paramount Chief of Shia, Togbe Dadzawa III, came to Newcastle in full regalia with fifteen members of his entourage to check her out. Fortunately they very pleased with what they found!

We had a civil wedding ceremony at Matfen Hall, an old country house in Northumberland, followed by Holy Matrimony over at the Catholic church in the village in Ghana. We had 150 guests eating lamb shanks at the service for the UK wedding and 1,500 eating whole lambs (some of which were presented to us live as wedding gifts) in Ghana! Five chiefs from different villages in Ghana attended and some had walked for six hours over mountains to get there.

Elaine was totally overwhelmed but very honoured that the village asked her to join the tribal council, and as I now have so many other commitments with Madventurer helping villages all over the world, she has taken over some of my responsibilities in developing Shia and engaging the youth in its development.

Elaine also now heads up the Mad Foundation, to help fund any stand-alone projects, and I concentrate on the travel business. We now both have two lives that we lead on different sides of the world and are very dedicated to giving back to projects which help move people forward overseas, and to providing access to experiences that help people develop through travel.

When I had my enforced leave of absence from university I had no clue what to do with my life, but it was the best thing that ever happened to me. To anyone thinking about taking time off for a gap year, I'd say go for it. Everyone grows once they step outside of their comfort zone. I now make it a policy to do something that makes me uncomfortable every day. Plus once a year I do a big project that takes me right out of my comfort zone. Before I went to Ghana I'd never done anything more adventurous than handing out fliers on the high street. Now I'll take two months off every year to do something like trekking in Antarctica or skydiving. That's the only way to grow.

I'm lucky – Madventurer has just celebrated its 100th big project abroad, and we've had very few mishaps beyond building a composting toilet that no one used (for quite obvious reasons).

But I don't mind making mistakes as long as I can learn from them. One year myself and a friend drove a Landrover to Ghana and rolled it in Mali. The driver was flown back to Britain with a broken leg and I had to finish the journey, through twenty police blocks, covered in bandages and driving a vehicle with neither glass nor lights. Another time, I broke my back skydiving. Fortunately I recovered from both those incidents and came out stronger as a result.

Mistakes are what help you learn and grow. If I'd never fallen down that storm drain in Accra, Madventurer would never have started and I'd never have done half the things I've done today. You have to take the risks and seize the opportunities. Don't think about it. Just do it.

CASEBOOK TWO: STEPHANIE LEE, THAI–BURMESE BORDER
Beryl Lee, 61, runs the charity set up by her daughter
'Steph's gap year changed thouands of lives.'

There's a Buddhist saying that you don't measure someone's life in terms of age, but in terms of what they've achieved. That's why one of the teachers at the Burmese refugee camp where our daughter Stephanie is buried told me, 'I want you to know, Steph died a very old lady.' She was just twenty-one, but she'd already accomplished so much that she's been written into the history books of the people she set out to help. And 4,000 mourners turned out for her funeral. How many of us could ever hope to have such an effect on others, however long we lived?

People have suggested to me that if Stephanie had never gone travelling, she'd never have died. My view is that if you've never gone travelling, you've never really lived.

Steph had just turned eighteen when she set off for her placement with GAP Activities, teaching in Hanoi for six months. She was a volunteer teacher at a school there – typically of her she'd wanted to go somewhere she'd never been before, rather than the more well-worn gap year destinations. At the end of it, she decided to backpack through Southeast Asia. She was always an independent spirit, an adventurer. Her route took her through Vietnam and up through Thailand. On 25 February 1999, my birthday, I had a phone call from her. 'I'm just about to get on a bus to go to Mae Hong Son,' she told me. 'I'll be travelling for a couple of days so I wanted to say "happy birthday" before I started out.' She told me she'd be home in a couple of months' time.

Instead, the following Monday I woke up to find her standing by my bed. During that bus journey something had happened that would change her life – and ours – forever. She'd got talking to a university lecturer from Singapore who was writing about the situation in Burma. He invited her to visit a refugee camp with him on the Thai–Burmese border near Mae Hong Son. The camp was home to the Karenni people who were fleeing human rights persecution in Burma, and had been given sanctuary in Thailand. As soon as she'd arrived there, she'd known that she wanted to help in any way she could. 'Mum, it's their sheer determination to educate their children in the face of such adversity,' she told me, her eyes bright with feeling. 'They don't really want to accept charity but have no choice. They just want their children to have the chance to learn to read and write and learn.'

Steph had been so affected by what she saw in the camp that she'd cut short her gap year trip and returned to the UK to set up a charity to raise funds to help the many children orphaned as a result of the brutality in Burma. She'd decided to build an orphanage, thereby giving them a home while they attended school in the camp. She'd given the Karenni an assurance that she'd be back at the camp by 1 May. She was, as ever, true to her word. Two months after returning to the UK, she flew back to Thailand with 500 kg of books, stationery and other much-needed equipment. True to form, she managed to persuade BA to fly it free of charge. Also true to form, she bluffed her way through Thai customs. 'I wore my shortest mini skirt,' she told me later. From May until September 1999, she stayed in the camp, teaching at the school. She was full of admiration for the Karenni people and their determination not to be defeated by the dire circumstances they found themselves in.

'Do you know, we have fourteen- and fifteen-year-olds here who have had next to no education in their lives but are desperate to come and learn to read,' she told me.

People always ask us, weren't we worried about her, being so young and in such a volatile part of the world – Burma is notoriously secretive and hostile to any form of foreign intervention, while the Thais are none too keen on having thousands of Burmese refugees on their borders. And of course we were worried, any parent would be. But we also knew our daughter and we knew there was no point trying to dissuade her from doing anything she'd set her heart on. Steph was a rebel, and a bit of an anarchist. If she could see a way of doing something, she'd do it. She was also a terrific motivator and a tremendous people person. If anyone was feeling down, they could rely on Steph to cheer them up.

My husband, Steve, and I flew over to visit her that first summer she was working in the camp and from the first day we were there, we could see why she was doing what she was doing. The refugees all live in the camp with checkpoints on the gate. Everything happens within the camp – the schools, the medical centre, camp administration, etc. The refugees are not allowed to leave the camp for any reason. There was one day we were out there with her when the camp came under attack by the Burmese army and some refugees were killed. I remember saying to her, 'If there's another attack, you must promise me you'll run away and get to safety.' She just put her hands on her hips and said, 'Mother, I'd no more do that than I'd run away and leave you if you were in danger. These people are my family now, just as much as you are. No way would I abandon them.'

We realised then that that was her life now. These were her people. After that, we'd never have dreamed of trying to stop her.

Steph had been intending to go to art school after her gap year, but her experience in the camp prompted her to change her mind. She decided she wanted to do Southeast Asian Studies at SOAS in London. Typically, it didn't bother her that she'd missed the deadline for applying. She literally went and hammered at the door. In fact, I'm still in touch with her tutors and they talk about it to this day. 'I'll never forget this young girl showing up,' one of them told me recently. 'She was so passionate. How could we not give her a chance?'

Steph started her course at SOAS the autumn she came back, but she flew out to work at the camp every Christmas and every summer. Plus, of course, she fundraised year-round for the charity she'd set up to help the Karenni. For the third year of her degree course, she was supposed to go out to teach at a secondary school in Burma. But Steph knew that she'd mainly be teaching the kids of the military: the very people who were oppressing her friends at the refugee camp. It would have been intolerable for her, but, luckily, SOAS was advised that as she'd already earned a reputation as an activist, it wouldn't be safe for her to go to Burma anyway. Instead she was given special dispensation to spend the year at the refugee camp.

She left the UK at the beginning of July 2001, intending to be away for the next fifteen months. She was filled with excitement at all the things she'd be able to accomplish during that amount of time, but it wasn't to be.

On 3 November, my husband received a phone call from a Karenni leader and good friend of hers at the camp. I was away on business at the time, but Steph's older brother Andy was home. The poor friend had the wretched job of telling Steve that Steph was dead. She'd been a passenger on a motorbike coming back to the camp from Mae Hong Son. There were three of them on the bike when it skidded going round a bend. The three landed on soft undergrowth but, tragically, buried in the undergrowth was a concrete marker post. Steph hit her head on it and died instantly from a broken neck. It was one of those fluke accidents.

The two boys, both refugee students of hers, got up and walked away with only a few bruises. Of course, that's not to say they didn't suffer terribly from what happened. The driver has been ostracised by the community, but we always make a point of going to see him and his family whenever we're over at the camp. They're suffering in the same way we are.

I was in Derbyshire when Steve rang to tell me the news. I just couldn't believe it. I'd only been out there just three weeks before, visiting Steph to take her a laptop computer. It seemed so unreal. In fact, it still seems so unreal – probably more so as she wasn't living at home at the time, so it wasn't as if she left one morning and failed to come home that night.

When she died, we were in the middle of moving house from northwest London to Lincolnshire. Steph had packed all her stuff away before she left. 'My whole life is packed in four tea chests,' she'd commented at the time. Well, those chests are still here, sealed up as she left them. We haven't had the guts to open them yet.

There was never any question for us that Steph should be buried anywhere but at the refugee camp. We didn't feel the need for her to be buried physically nearby. We felt she was with us in our hearts, and alive to us in so many different ways. As you can imagine, there was a lot of red tape involved in burying her in the refugee camp in Thailand and we had to go to the British embassy in Bangkok before being able to go up to Mae Hong Son. When we arrived there, we first had to go to the hospital to identify her body. Steve and Andy did that. I just couldn't face it. The next day some Karenni women were allowed down to the hospital to prepare her body and dress her in Karenni costume and then we took her to the camp.

Nothing could have prepared us for what greeted us there. Thousands of people lined the dirt road into the camp. Her students were waiting for her, all smartly dressed in clean white shirts, and they hoisted her coffin onto their shoulders and carried her to the school hall which had been converted into a memorial for Steph. A huge banner hung across the room reading: 'Memorial service for Donor and Philanthropist Stephanie Lee'. The whole room was decked out in flowers and candles, and as soon as we arrived with her coffin, they opened it and surrounded Stephanie with flowers too. The traditional Karenni funeral rites went on round the clock for twenty-four hours. There's a tradition that no one should leave the coffin, so they performed endless songs and dances in that hall in an outpouring of love and affection.

We felt completely overwhelmed, but somehow, the following day, during her funeral service, I managed to give a speech in which I reassured the orphans Steph had been raising money for that even though Steph was no longer there, her work would go on.

Afterwards, we began the three-mile funeral procession from the school to the cemetery. Again we were overwhelmed. The entire route was lined with refugees – thousands of them, all waiting to pay a last tribute to Stephanie. We walked with the coffin the whole way along the jungle track through the rainforest and up to the top of the mountain. It had rained the night before, and at points I was up to my knees in mud, but it didn't matter. Behind and in front of us, as far as the eye could see, was an endless procession of people, many playing traditional musical instruments, all here to say goodbye to our daughter. It was one of the most moving things we've ever seen. These are people who have nothing, but they'd all dressed up as best as they could – children, old people, everyone. The coffin was carried by her students. At various stages along the route, a new team of pallbearers would take over, all wearing fresh white shirts. The organisation and planning that went into it was incredible.

We arrived at the special cemetery where the Karenni bury their dignitaries. That's how much they thought of Stephanie – that she's buried alongside the last president. Overnight they'd built her a concrete tomb and one of the Christian priests from the camp performed the burial, although all of the other religious groups were also involved. It was the first time they'd had a funeral service where every religion – Christianity, Buddhism and animism – was involved. She'd simply touched the lives of everyone there and everyone wanted to be part of it.

Even though Stephanie's insurance policy would have covered the cost of the funeral, the refugees there insisted on paying for the whole thing themselves. They'd gone round the whole camp and everyone had given a donation, even if it was just a baht (worth one and a half pence). Some had given up their rice rations for the funeral feast. It was their way of paying tribute.

I never got a chance to say a private goodbye to Stephanie, but it didn't worry me. I always felt she was as much theirs as she was ours. Even now when we go to see her grave, we're never alone. There's always a party atmosphere there. The Karenni go up there for her birthday and on the anniversary of her death and light hundreds of candles. They send us photos – it's the most beautiful sight.

We stayed at the camp for a further ten days, carried forward by the whole euphoria of the funeral. It didn't hit us until much later that Stephanie wasn't coming back. In fact, I think it probably still hasn't properly hit us. You never get over losing a child. It's not what nature intended. It's like losing your future. We wonder what she'd be doing now. You see her colleagues moving on, developing, getting married, all the things she'll never get to do. I never wear mascara anymore because, even five years on, hardly a day goes by without me shedding a tear for Steph. But it's really me I'm feeling sorry for, not her. I know she isn't suffering.

The thing that has really helped most has been continuing the work that Stephanie started at the camp. I now spend about five months of the year over there and I think I'll probably end up living there full time someday. I feel happier over there than I do here in England, and closer to Steph. Sometimes when I listen to people in this country complaining about not having a new car or whatever, I despair. When you've lived with people who have nothing in life but who have such fortitude and are happy with so little, you feel we're so spoiled. Here kids have every opportunity for education and don't take it, while out there are children who are desperate for every crumb of education they can get.

Don't get me wrong, I'm not a do-gooder. I get a real buzz out of what we're doing out in Thailand. It gives me a tremendous feeling of satisfaction, being able to make a vast difference to someone's life. Not many people have that opportunity. I'm really grateful to Stephanie for giving me that chance.

A lot of people have said to me, 'I bet you wish Stephanie had never decided to take a gap year.' Nothing could be further from the truth. Although we've lost Steph, I'd much rather she'd achieved what she did in a short time than stayed here in a humdrum job and never achieved anything that made her happy.

To any other parents worrying about gap years, I'd say, 'Just let your children go. They've got to experience life and the world. The more young people who go out and do that, the better place the world will be.' At the end of the day, your child could walk out of the door in Manchester or Birmingham and be hit by a bus. You don't stop your life just because of something that *might* happen.

Life is for living. We never know what is going to happen next. Stephanie taught me that.

Stephanie's charity is called the Karenni Student Development Programme (KSDP; registered charity no. 1108288). For more information contact Beryl on ksdp.uk@lineone.net or visit www.karennisu.org where you can read more about the Karenni.

CASEBOOK THREE: SARAH CUMMING, THAILAND
Sarah Cumming, 23, London
'Surviving the tsunami just made me want to travel more.'

For as long as I can remember, I wanted to see the world. I was curious and wanted to see every country and every kind of landscape on the planet. My original gap year itinerary included nearly thirty countries but when I began to research more thoroughly, I realized I was being a little ambitious. By the time I finally booked the ticket my plan was to travel around Southeast Asia, learning to dive, then go on to New Zealand and Australia, and southern Africa. I intended to finish my travels with a few months in Kenya or Tanzania teaching English. I reckon I stuck to less than half of that original itinerary. So much for advance planning!

I set off in October 2004. Although I'd actually left Portsmouth University a year before that, I'd spent the time working as an administrator, raising money for my trip. First stop was Hong Kong, then on to Thailand. On the idyllic island of Phi Phi I made loads of friends and fell in love with scuba diving, despite not being very confident in the water. I was supposed to fly to Australia in December but changed all my plans so I could stay on Phi Phi to study to become a dive instructor.

The course was great and I loved every second of it. Although I was working hard, Christmas in Thailand was great fun. A vibrant atmosphere day and night and plenty of sun. If paradise did exist, then this had to be it. At around 10.30 the morning of the 26th, Boxing Day, I was still in bed in my bungalow, having rolled in at 7.30 that morning from the Christmas celebrations. Still half asleep, I had a bleary chat with my friend Freddie from the dive course who was sharing my room. Then I dropped back off to sleep for another ten minutes.

Suddenly I was woken up by this tremendous noise. At first I tried to ignore it – I was used to a lot of noise from the metal trolleys they sometimes pushed up and down outside the bungalow. But after a while I started to get angry – I needed to sleep!

The noise was getting louder and closer. It sounded like a train about to derail and crash straight into my bungalow. It was Freddie's eyes that first told me something was seriously wrong. Freddie got up to look out of the window. Then he turned round to face me with an expression of shock on his face, but he had no time to say anything. Behind him, I saw the wall of our bungalow starting to cave in, from the bottom up. Bizarrely, I still thought it was a train – although what a train would be doing on the island I didn't think to ask.

As the wall collapsed I thought I was going to die. Then I was being sucked backwards. I was trying to grab hold of anything in the room to stop me going backwards, but I think something in the room must have hit me. I felt like I was being sucked into an underwater cave.

Then the whole room collapsed on top of me. I was still under the water. I couldn't make sense of it. I just kept thinking to myself, 'I need to get out.' When I'd run out of air and tried to breathe and swallowed water instead, I really thought that was it. It was weird. Half of me was calmly thinking 'I'm dying' and the other half was fighting to live. I wasn't scared but I was angry that I was going to die on a Boxing Day, so every Christmas from then on would be ruined for my family. Also, they'd be left with my £10,000 student loan. The injustice of it made me really cross. It sounds insane but I remember worrying about whether my dead body should be found with mouth and eyes open or closed. If I opened them, at least my parents would know I died fighting to live, but then if I closed them, they'd know I died peacefully.

All the time I was clawing at the bricks on top of me. I had no idea which way was up. Then I remembered that if I was confused on a dive, all I had to do was blow bubbles and watch which direction they went. Somehow, from somewhere deep within my lungs, I produced a couple of bubbles that probably saved my life. I knew which way was up now. Finally, as I had almost no fight left in me, I moved a brick and felt some air.

I launched myself upwards and grabbed onto something. It was a tree. Fear kicked in then. All I could see, all round me, was water, the tops of trees and a lot of floating debris. There were no people. I didn't know whether I was alive or dead. It took a few minutes to refill my body with oxygen. I felt weak and dizzy. I was convinced Freddie couldn't have survived. I wasn't even sure if I had survived.

As I hung on, the thought came forcefully into my head: 'I will not drown today.' I repeated this thought out loud until I was safe. I knew I had to get to land and launched myself across the water, grabbing onto trees, but the water kept taking me back towards the sea. I was being slammed into things and watched helplessly as the bodies of two dead Thai people were also battered against trees.

My only thought now was for survival. I knew I had to protect myself as best I could, so I put my knees up to my chin and my hands covering my face. This tactic paid off, as most of my injuries were on my legs and arms.

As I became more aware of the dangers, I realised that freeing myself from my bungalow was the easy part. The fear rose in me as I was pulled further towards the sea. When the water started to go out, it revealed tree roots. I realised if I could grab onto them I had a chance of avoiding being swept right out.

The water was about waist deep as it was going out and I grabbed the first tree root desperately, only to find it came uprooted in my hand, so I made a lunge for the next one and the same thing happened. In this fashion I made my way along the sea shore until I reached the reservoir channel – a ditch that links the nearby reservoir with the sea. I knew there was no way to cross it without being sucked under and crushed by the debris.

Hauling myself up onto a rock, I thought, 'I don't know what to do now.' I knew I had two choices. Either I'd be rescued, or I'd die. Luckily for me I got rescued. There was a resort a bit higher up in the town from the hotel where I'd been staying and I could see people standing up by the swimming pool, calling to me to go back the way I'd come. But I had no more energy left. I was exhausted. All I could do was sit on the rock.

Suddenly, one of the guys from the resort jumped into the water, grabbing onto a mattress that was floating there. He managed to push the mattress over to me, and gestured to me to get on, but I didn't want to. The thought of getting back into that water was just too much. But he kept on trying to persuade me. He even took off his T-shirt and gave it to me, which is when I realised I was completely naked.

Eventually we both got onto the mattress. We were tossed backwards and forward and eventually got washed up near the resort where some Thai guys managed to get us out. I think they carried me off wrapped in towels. I kept saying, 'I can't believe I'm alive,' which really surprised them as they'd had no idea of the extent of the devastation where I'd just come from.

'Everyone's dead,' I told them, because I was so sure no one could have survived. 'All my friends are dead.'

'Big wave came and covered island,' they said.

The hotel had a medical box and the people at the resort cleaned up my feet as best they could, but I had lots of other wounds that weren't seen at that point. They tried to make me eat and drink, but I couldn't face it.

Then other people started to come from the same direction I'd arrived. Many were in far worse shape than me. Some had even lost limbs. The hotel lobby became a mini hospital.

Soon after that I fainted. When I came to, I'd been carried into a bungalow near the reception area. Because of the pain everywhere, I could only lie on one side. Looking down, I was taken aback to see that the whole bed was black. I'd been covered in black mud from the water. For weeks afterwards, I was struggling to remove the mud from my hair where it had mixed with brick cement and solidified.

The guy who had saved me came to see how I was. He'd gone back into the water to rescue more people after me. That was the thing about the tsunami, so many people did heroic things for people they didn't even know.

Then came a warning that a third wave was coming. At this point I got really scared. I couldn't face going through all that again. We all knew we had to get to higher ground. As I couldn't walk, some guys carried me halfway up the mountain. They put me down next to a big water tank where I spent the next eighteen hours. I was with a few people I'd never met before but they did a good job of looking after me that night as I literally couldn't move.

Some time later, some Thai people came round offering medical aid. I knew I was hurting but I couldn't tell where the worst of the pain was, so again the most severe wounds went untreated. It wasn't their fault. There were so many people to treat, they were really overwhelmed. I kept saying, 'I think there are more,' but as I couldn't really move, I couldn't show them where they were.

The following morning the helicopter arrived to take the wounded off to hospital. Some Swedish guys put me on a door and carried me to the helicopter. They'd been up all night ferrying injured people around. There were so many people who did everything they could to help others. They just didn't stop.

It was while I was being carried from the mountain to the helicopter that I got the first sense of the devastation the tsunami had caused, seeing the bodies and the destruction and damage. The island had practically disappeared.

The forty-five-minute helicopter journey to the hospital on the mainland was very emotional. I wanted to stay on the island and search for my friends, but knew I couldn't. I arrived at the hospital at 9 am on 27 December. I still felt that I was more badly hurt than I realised, but there were so many injured people there – mostly lying on the floor. I knew was one of the lucky ones.

I wanted to phone home straight away, to let my family know I was okay. It was 10.30 am Thai time, but only 4 am at home. At first no one answered. I thought, 'Either they haven't heard about what's happened, or they're already on a flight over.'

Eventually my sister answered. I said, 'Tell Mum and Dad I'm okay. I'll be home as soon as possible.'

I can only imagine the relief my family must have felt. My parents had found out about the tsunami just three hours after it happened. I'd been hoping that, as they didn't normally watch TV over Christmas, they wouldn't have heard about it, but of course they did. The guilt I feel about what I put my friends and family through that day remains one of the hardest things to deal with.

I sent a group email from the hospital to everyone I knew telling them I was alive. I was so high on painkillers and adrenaline that I think the email I sent made people laugh as well as cry.

As soon as I could move, or rather, be carried, I started searching the hospital for my friends. I'd heard reports of survivors from the resort where I'd been, so I was hoping against hope that I'd find someone I knew. Incredibly, I found Freddie. He was lying on the floor, facing away from me. I shouted his name and tried to move towards him, but my legs wouldn't work, so in the end I crawled over to him.

'I thought you were dead!' I said over and over, giving him a big hug.

Miraculously, all the people from the dive shop were alive and well. I was so relieved that none of my close friends had died, but sad to hear that some of the Thai people we'd met hadn't made it.

I spent most of my time in the hospital with an English guy whose girlfriend was missing. I told him not to give up hope. I mean, hadn't I believed that all my friends were dead and yet they'd all turned up alive? Tragically, my new friend wasn't so lucky. Nine months after the tsunami, the body of his missing girlfriend was identified.

I spent one night in the hospital itself and the next night was transferred to a makeshift hospital, which was a hotel down the road. That's where I discovered the more serious wounds I hadn't found before, which by this time had become infected. I was lying on the floor along with about 100 other people. I was searching for injuries with my hands when my hand went right into my leg. I thought, 'Hang on, that's not right!' But I couldn't get up to tell anyone. I had to wait several hours before the nurses came round to change my dressings again.

I stayed in the hotel waiting for the British embassy to show up and let me know what to do, but no one arrived. In the end I was told, 'The embassy isn't coming. You need to make your way to Bangkok.' Bear in mind I still couldn't walk at this stage. I thought, 'That's going to be interesting.'

Luckily, free flights were laid on to Bangkok and I managed to arrange to get on one. Once in Bangkok I was taken to a hotel where I spent the night being looked after by other English people. Then I was taken to the hospital. Medical staff there wanted to admit me for a week, but by this stage I'd had enough. I just wanted to get home. I promised that I'd go straight to hospital when I got back to England and they let me go.

After that one night in the Bangkok hotel, I managed to get to the airport and get on a flight back to Heathrow. I had been told it would be a free flight, but when I arrived at the airport I couldn't get on that one, so my dad had to pay £600 for me to get back. Then I couldn't get a seat on the plane. Because of my injuries I needed an aisle seat, but none of the cabin crew would take me seriously. I think they thought I was drunk. In the end some kind guy gave up his aisle seat and took the middle one instead. In fact, he kept me sane on the journey home.

When we arrived at Heathrow, we were kept on the plane for an hour while the authorities checked who we were. Obviously, most people didn't have papers or passports, so it was all a bit of a mess.

On arrival I panicked. I didn't want to get off the plane and see my parents. Even though they still had no idea what had happened to me, I felt too guilty about everything I'd put them through. And I knew there'd probably be photographers there, which I really couldn't face.

I was carried off the plane and put onto one of those airport buggy things, but I made them drop me just before the door into arrivals. It felt important that my family could see me walking. I took two tottering steps through into the arrivals hall and then stopped. I couldn't have gone any further. Luckily my sister spotted me and ran through the barriers to hug me, then my parents did the same. After that I was taken through a door away from the photographers and smuggled off to the car park.

Getting home was the best feeling ever. The Christmas decorations were still up and I can still remember how good that first cup of tea tasted. That feeling of euphoria lasted for the next three weeks. I was living on adrenaline. Everything felt great. But I knew even then I wouldn't stay home long. The first thing my parents asked me was when I was going back. They knew me too well. 'As soon as I can walk,' I replied.

Although my natural high stemmed the pain for a while, as my body started healing I could feel the pain from my infected wounds. My whole body was swollen and I had a lovely black eye. I'm surprised anyone recognised me. I couldn't walk very well and I'd pulled all the muscles in my arms grabbing onto the tree roots. I couldn't shower or take a bath for five weeks.

Gradually the euphoria wore off and I started getting itchy feet – and not just because of the scabs! I felt a real need to go back and pick up where I left off.

In March 2005 I went back to Thailand. At first I felt fine returning to Phi Phi and to the bare remains of the bungalow where I'd been staying. Incredibly, I even managed to find some of my stuff that had been buried under the bricks for three months. But then, as I was enjoying a drink in a bar only a few hours after I'd arrived back, the band stopped playing and there was an announcement. 'There's been an earthquake.'

Taking no chances, I ran for my life. I waited up the mountain until the all clear was finally given at 4 am. Many people left the island the next day, so great was the fear of any kind of repeat of what had happened before, but I was determined to stay and help the people who had helped me. I stayed for a few weeks, helping with the rebuilding.

In April, I left Thailand to pick up my travel plans where I'd left off. But I couldn't shake off the memories. I loved Thailand. I would have loved it anyway, even if nothing had happened there, but because of the tsunami I felt a particular bond with it. I still do. In October 2005 I was back again. This time I was stronger, although still not completely physically recovered, and could be more help volunteering and cleaning up. I also finished my dive master course there and worked as a dive master for a few months in the same centre where I'd done my training. It was a great achievement for me – I was so glad I could still get in the water.

I stayed in Thailand until Christmas 2005 – the anniversary of the tsunami. After all that time I don't think I was really prepared for how much the one-year memorial service would affect me, but it brought a lot of painful memories flooding back. I saw pictures of the victims and realised I had met many of them as customers of the dive shop or friends of friends. Seeing the grief of those who lost people was overwhelming and I knew it was time to leave and do my best to move on. After that, it was on to India for a couple of months before returning home in March 2006.

Now I'm working for a publishing company in London. It feels so strange to be doing a nine-to-five job after travelling for so long. Thailand is never far from my thoughts. Most of my injuries are healed now, but I have a few nice scars and holes and my ankle isn't great. I still have nightmares about what happened. But if I ever find myself wallowing in self-pity and thinking 'this has ruined my life', I give myself a little shake. Because I'm still here. I'm still living.

I think I always was a strong person emotionally, but now I feel like I can handle literally anything. That's not to say I'm superwoman or anything. I've lost a little bit of innocence now – I know the unexpected can happen any time, and any of us could die at any time. But that's just made me determined to live life more fully.

People often ask me whether what happened to me has put me off travelling, but nothing could be less true. My time abroad has made me into the person I am now. I'm already planning my next trip. I'd say to everyone: 'Don't let anything put you off a gap year. Bad things can happen anywhere – in London, in Munich, in France. Go out. See the world. Live.'

CASEBOOK FOUR: SHELDON WARNICK, CAMBODIA
Sheldon Warnick, 19, Roehampton
'Despite the corruption, mugging and a nasty motorbike accident, I loved my gap year.'

People look at me like I'm crazy when I say I loved my gap year. After all, I had a placement in what turned out to be a corrupt orphanage in Cambodia, then came home on crutches with my leg ripped open after a motorbike accident. But you know, at the same time, I got to know a different country, I experienced the pleasure that comes with travelling alone, with no ties or responsibilities, I met fantastic people and I learned a lot about myself. How could anyone not love that?

When I finished school, I signed up to teach English with an organisation that runs voluntary projects abroad. I'd already done some TEFL training, so I knew I could do it. I picked on Cambodia by getting a map out and literally jabbing a finger down. My plan was to teach for a month and then travel for two, before going on to South America.

I was placed in an orphanage run by a minister's wife. Right away I realised something was wrong. The orphanage gets a lot of money from donations and grants, but none of it was going to the children. The children were underfed and living and sleeping in awful conditions. They all had illnesses – typhoid, hepatitis, cholera. Some, unfortunately, had AIDS and all had ear, nose and eye infections. It was quite shocking.

Allegedly, I was told, Gary Glitter had been to this orphanage, posing as a medical doctor and taking children out to 'examine' them. I don't know if it is true, but that's the kind of place it was.

I'd been expecting a proper school where I could start teaching straight away, but there was just a hut with open sides. The blackboard had a big hole in the middle so you couldn't write on it.

The organisation that had sent me had never had a volunteer working at this particular orphanage. In fact, I was among the first volunteers they'd ever sent to Cambodia, so they had no idea what this place was like. I informed them about everything, but there wasn't much they could do. They were in a difficult position – obviously they didn't want to just pull their volunteer out, as it would leave the kids with nothing. But as long as there's a volunteer there from an official organisation, tourists assume it's a bona fide orphanage and give donations – none of which reach the kids.

I set up a classroom to do some basic English teaching. I paid for books and whiteboards out of my own pocket. I tried to make it a warm, cosy environment for them, but it's hard when they're not getting proper food or sleep.

The kids were lovely, though, really strong. If they fell, they just got straight back up again. And even though they were eating less than a street cat would here, they still thanked me for teaching them.

Right from the beginning I decided not to get wound up by the injustice there, because there was nothing I could do about it. You have to try not to get too involved or else you'd never be able to leave. There was a volunteer there who got in way too deep and couldn't afford to leave and she was breaking down from the stress of it.

Even though I tried my best not to get attached, I couldn't help it. But I knew I was only staying a month and I knew it would be really hard to leave. I think the easiest thing for the kids is to tell them from the start that you're only going to be staying a short time, and then to gradually fade away rather than having a big emotional farewell. If you cry, it makes them cry and it's not fair to put them through that every month when someone else goes.

In the end, the only way I could bring myself to leave was to tell myself: 'I had a contract with this organisation and I completed it.' And that's the truth. At the end of the day, I'm just a nineteen-year-old student who'd finished his placement. What could I do? I handed the problem back to the people who'd sent me. I told them they had a moral obligation to sort it out.

After the stress of the orphanage it was a relief to go travelling. I know you're supposed to have a plan when you go travelling, but I didn't, so the result was I did a lot of back-tracking and time-wasting, but I also experienced the thrill of turning up somewhere and asking, 'Excuse me, where am I?' One time I got stuck and had to walk for two days and spend two nights out on the road, but it was great. Scary, but great.

I had a friend with me for a week and a half, but apart from that I travelled alone and really recommend it. You always meet people and you end up tagging along with loads of people instead of being stuck with a partner or a group. I travelled with a Canadian couple for a week, and hooked up with a group from New Zealand for a while. I also got to experience staying with local people. Travelling alone gives you so much flexibility.

I did have one incident where I was mugged. It was when I was with a friend. We were stupidly carrying all our money – around $500 - in our money belts, instead of just carrying a decoy amount there and keeping the rest somewhere else.

We'd been to the foreign exchange (tip to travellers: when you go in and out of any money-changing facility, make sure you're not followed). Some people came after us and my friend had a knife put to his neck. At the same time I felt a sharp object in my back. My friend started getting his wallet out and as he was doing it, the guy behind me snatched my money bag off my waist and they ran away.

It was all over so quickly. As soon as they'd gone we started laughing from nerves. The thing about things like that is, sure they're a pain, but when they're over, they're over. You just have to move on. When you're travelling you stop taking everything so seriously. When a five-hour journey ends up taking twelve hours, you just accept it, you give into it.

My motorbike accident happened towards the end of my time in Cambodia. To be really honest, tourists aren't allowed to drive vehicles in Cambodia at all, but of course everyone ignores that rule. In fact, drivers in Cambodia ignore every rule. I don't think you need a licence to drive a scooter there, so no one ever bothers to learn the rules of the road and the result is chaos with traffic going in all directions and people doing all sorts of illegal, often suicidal, manoeuvres.

I was driving and I came to a junction where there was a silver car in the middle of the road. I had to swerve to try to go around it, but as I did so it carried on moving and hit me side on, trapping my leg under the bike.

This is where it starts to get a little surreal because the driver of the car suffered a heart attack, leaving me to deal with her son-in-law. I was taken by taxi to a nearby hospital, accompanied by the police and the driver's son-in-law. My foot was torn right up to the ankle and the skin was hanging off. They had to put it back, sew it together and then give me a massive dose of antibiotics to stave off any infection. I was told to stay in the hospital, but there was a hotel close by that was much nicer to be in, and cheaper than the hospital – $10 dollars a night, compared to $20 for a hospital bed.

The son-in-law and I had to go to the police station to pay to get his car and my moped out. As neither of us had any insurance (mine had run out after my work-stay period ended and, sod's law, I hadn't thought I'd be needing to extend it), the driver's family was held responsible and had to pay all the 'expenses'. This included healthcare for me for a week, plus the fee to get the vehicles back and then the bribe to the police.

Bribes vary in Cambodia. If you're randomly stopped by the police for driving a vehicle, they'll usually ask for about $10, but sometimes you can get away with just buying them a Coke – it depends. After the crash, the driver's family had to pay a $55 bribe, which is quite a lot when you consider top-level police officers only earn about $50 a month.

The accident has put an end to my travelling for a while. I had to go home to recuperate. As the wound dressing needs changing regularly and I was on crutches, there didn't seem any point in staying abroad. But it certainly hasn't put me off travelling. In fact, I'm already planning to continue my trip to South America as planned, just as soon as my foot heals. I'm hoping to fit some teaching in Nicaragua around starting a course at Roehampton University, so as you can tell, the experience in the Cambodian orphanage hasn't put me off either.

In fact, I'd advise anyone to take a gap year and to do some kind of voluntary placement. It's a great way of getting involved with a country and feeling connected with the people. It's an unrepeatable experience.

CASEBOOK FIVE: POLLY AKED,
SOUTH AFRICA
Polly Aked, 21, Aberystwyth
'After delivering a baby in the street, I can do anything!'

I always knew going to teach in South Africa for my gap year would give me some terrific memories and exciting experiences, but I never thought that I'd end up delivering a baby on the side of the road in one of Knysna's townships!

On Thursday, 30 March 2006, I finished school early, at noon, so I decided to take a local minibus taxi back to the volunteer house. About a minute into the ride, a heavily pregnant woman got on, with a one-year-old child strapped to her back. She was talking quite quickly, in Xhosa, and the driver explained that she was in labour and he was going to take her to the hospital. My first reaction was, 'Oh, I hope she's okay,' but as another minute went by, and she yelled at the driver to stop, I thought, 'Oh no, she's going to have the baby now!'

We stopped at the side of the road and she handed me her now screaming baby who had been on her back. The two other men stayed inside the taxi. I got out along with the driver and watched her lie down. We were in a really remote area of the township, and no one was coming out of their shacks. She then lifted her skirt and I could immediately tell that she was fully dilated! I started panicking when the driver told me that I would have to deliver the baby.

A woman eventually emerged from her shack and saw what was going on. She disappeared and came back moments later with a bowl of water, many towels and a pair of scissors. Relief washed over me. 'Finally, someone who knows what they are doing!' I thought. But as she started talking to the driver in Xhosa again, he told me that the 'new' woman would look after the mother and that I would *still* have to deliver the child. With my mouth wide open in shock, I tried to explain that I was by no means qualified or capable of doing this. I'm so clumsy I'm not even allowed into a shop that sells glass stuff unless my hands are firmly in my pockets – let alone deliver a baby! They'd got the wrong person.

But as the woman screamed and I saw under her skirt that the head was crowning, I automatically dropped to my knees, put the other baby down, and tried desperately to remember everything I had seen on TV shows like *ER*. The taxi driver, who did an excellent job translating, told her that I wanted her to push – and she did. By now I had lots of towels over me and the other woman started pouring warm water over the patient's belly, although I'm not sure why. An older lady came over and sang to the mother and held her hand, leaving me to focus on delivering – a baby!

When she pushed, half of the head came out, and I started crying, along with the mother and her other baby. I asked her to push again and she shook her head, but I was worried it couldn't breathe in the vaginal canal, and not knowing any medical details, I begged her to push again.

This time she pushed the baby out to its shoulders, and I could see how this widest part of the baby was hurting her. Another push got the baby to its waist and that's when I noticed that it wasn't crying. I didn't know if this was normal, but I gave her time to rest. In one hand I held the baby in a towel, while with the other I felt around inside her. By this time I had blood and gunk all over me, but all I could think of was that this baby was not yet crying… I figured it would take one more push for the legs to come out, but I didn't know if I would have to pull it out or it would just 'pop' out!

So much was going on that it was hard to focus. Not to

mention that I had the Diana Ross song 'Baby Love' going on replay in my head. I kept trying to think, 'What comes next? What do I do now?' but all I could think back to was an old episode of *The Fresh Prince of Bel-Air* when Will Smith delivered a baby in the back of a limousine, so I changed my line of thinking to: 'What would Will Smith do?'

When she was finally ready to give a last push, I prepared for the whole baby to come out. With that last big push, I was crying as well, as I suddenly had this beautiful, messy little boy in my hands! I started to panic when he didn't cry and I didn't know whether or not to smack him to make him cry, but thankfully he let out a wail shortly afterwards and I breathed a sigh of relief!

I knew that in the movies they'd now get the mucus out of the nose and mouth, but I didn't have the utensils, so I got a corner of a towel and got out as much as possible. I started wiping the baby off and realised how messy everything was. The woman who'd helped me brought her scissors out and started to cut at the umbilical cord. Throughout the whole delivery I hadn't been too freaked out by all that had gone on, but I had to turn my head at this!

Once she was finished, I remembered that the mother would now have to push out the placenta, and while still holding the baby, I told her to push again. Exhausted as she was, she did. The older woman took it away and I still don't know what happened to it, but I don't think I really want to know!

I offered the baby to the mother, but she was too tired to even hold it, so I stared at this bundle of new life and started crying even more. When I eventually did pass the baby to her, she indicated that she wanted to feed him. I didn't think that you were supposed to do that for hours, but I helped her put the baby to her breast. I then returned to her other child, who was still crying, and took a look at my surroundings. I couldn't believe it!

I asked the driver to ask the mother what she would name him, suggesting 'Polly' as a joke, but she just laughed and said 'Dumsani'.

About half an hour went by, and we eventually convinced her to go to the hospital to get checked out. Once there, the nurse took the newborn and put the mother in a wheelchair. I still had her other child, now asleep in my arms, and asked if I should stay, but the nurse said it would be better if I left. The mother kept stroking my hand and face, saying, 'Thank you, thank you.' She said something else in Xhosa to me and the driver explained that she was saying, 'You're my angel, you're my angel,' something I will never forget.

When I left the hospital, I sat dumbfounded in the taxi. The driver said to me that I was told to deliver the baby because I was white and they thought I would know what I was doing. Still surprised, he told me I had done well, and that I wouldn't have to pay the 50p for the taxi ride! Cheers!

Looking back, I can't believe what happened. I realise now that I actually knew more about delivery than I had at first thought, and a lot of it comes down purely to a woman's instinct. I'm so proud of the fact that I didn't bail out when faced with the situation, and that all went well.

After I got back to where I was staying, I rushed in and told everyone, then called my parents. To say they were surprised would be an understatement! I remained in South Africa for four months and even though I didn't get to see the mother or baby again, I felt much more involved in township life because of what had happened and much more a part of the community.

The experience gave me so much confidence. I'm not the kind of person who deals well with frightening situations. I would normally have fled from the scene and let someone else deal with, but since I was the only person there, I had to act. I'm really proud of myself that I did it – I really pushed my boundaries. I think it's lucky that I just didn't have time to be nervous.

Nowadays, as a result of what happened in South Africa, I'm a lot braver and more willing to face up to challenges. Whenever faced with difficulties now, I try my best to give 100%. The idea that I helped a new life come into the world still baffles me. I'm just so happy that everything went well.

My gap year definitely changed me. I see my friends who went straight to university, and I wonder how they ever survived without having time to find out what really interests them. I met people who were so different from me, leading completely different lives. When I think about my time in South Africa, I remember how involved I was, how important my time there was, and it makes my life now seem quite trivial in comparison. Their poverty is still happening, their struggle is never-ending. But it's pointless feeling guilty about it. So I remember their smiles and look at the pictures. Hopefully I made an impact on their lives, just like they did on mine. And hopefully, if I save up enough money, I'll be going back there next year!

Delivering a baby is something I didn't expect to do in a lifetime, never mind on a voluntary placement in South Africa. It's an amazing story to tell, and a memory that I will have with me forever.

And the best thing of all is that, when people ask how my gap year trip went, I can nonchalantly say: 'Well, I rode a camel, taught kids for four months, met incredible people and, oh yeah, delivered a baby on the side of a dusty township road!'

USEFUL ADDRESSES

GAPYEAR.COM

Since its inception in 1998, gapyear.com has been offering anyone interested in taking a gap year support, advice, information and loads of opportunities for meeting fellow gappers.

The Gapyear Company Ltd
20 Chalfont Square
Old Foundry Road
Ipswich
Suffolk
IP4 2AJ

0870 241 6704
www.gapyear.com

GAP SPORTS

Specialists in combining sports volunteer projects with adventurous travel.

GAP SPORTS
Willowbank House
84 Station Road
Marlow
Bucks SL7 1NX

0870 837 9797
www.gapsports.com

GAP ACTIVITY PROJECTS

A not-for-profit organisation which specialises in voluntary work place-ments overseas for 17–25 year-olds.

44 Queen's Road
Reading
Berkshire
RG1 4BB

0118 959 4914
www.gap.org.uk

PROJECT TRUST

An educational charity that sends 18-year-olds overseas to spend twelve months living in local communities and working as volunteers.

The Hebridean Centre
Isle of Coll
Argyll
PA78 6TE

01879 230444
info@projecttrust.org.uk
www.projecttrust.org.uk

OUTREACH INTERNATIONAL

Runs small-scale, 'worthwhile' volunteering projects in Mexico, Cambodia, Costa Rica, Ecuador and the Galapagos Islands.

Bartlett's Farm
Hayes Road
Compton Dundon
Somerset
TA11 6PF

01458 274957
info@outreachinternational.co.uk
www.outreachinternational.co.uk

OBJECTIVE GAP SAFETY

Runs courses in safety awareness for young travellers.

Objective Travel Safety Ltd
Bragborough Lodge Farm

Braunston
Daventry
Northants
NN11 7HA

01788 899 029
www.objectivegapyear.com

i-2-i

Sends people on 'meaningful' volunteer projects to 24 destinations worldwide.

i-to-i UK
Woodside House
261 Low Lane
Leeds
LS18 5NY

0870 333 2332
info@i-to-i.com
www.i-to-i.com

AFRICA AND ASIA VENTURE

Combines travel and adventure with voluntary projects in local communities within Africa and Asia.

Africa and Asia Venture
10 Market Place
Devizes
Wiltshire
SN10 1HT

01380 729 009
av@aventure.co.uk
www.aventure.co.uk

Useful Addresses

STA TRAVEL

Provides tailor-made deals on flights
and other travel needs for young
travellers and students.

0207 361 6262
www.statravel.co.uk

MADVENTURER

Offers award-winning community
development projects and
adventures worldwide.

Mad HQ
1-4 Forth Lane,
Newcastle upon Tyne
NE1 5HX
United Kingdom

team@madventurer.com
www.madventurer.com
0845 121 1996

VSO – VOLUNTARY SERVICE OVERSEAS

One of the world's oldest volunteer
sending charities, VSO runs
numerous schemes for 18-25-year-
olds.

317 Putney Bridge Road
London
SW15 2PN

enquiries@vso.org.uk
www.vso.org.uk
020 8780 7200